Relationship Breakdown

A Survival Guide

Christina Basciano

WARD LOCK

To my mother and father,
who inspired this quest for enlightenment.
I wish you both peace.

A WARD LOCK BOOK

First published in the UK 1997
by Ward Lock
Wellington House
125 Strand
LONDON
WC2R 0BB

A Cassell Imprint

Distributed in the United States
by Sterling Publishing Co., Inc.
387 Park Avenue South, New York, NY 10016 – 8810

A British Library Cataloguing in Publication Data block for this book
may be obtained from the British Library

ISBN 0 7063 7609 9

Designed by Paula McCann
Printed and bound in Great Britain by CPD (Wales), Ebbw Vale

Contents

Acknowledgements

My grateful thanks to therapists Liz Morris and Tim Sparrow, who have consistently offered their wisdom, support and guidance since my work on relationship breakdown began. Their words of encouragement helped to keep the creative fires burning. Thanks also to Gordon Evans, Convener of the Scottish charity Break-up Support, who was the first to support my belief that this book should be written with a sense of realism and to suggest that it should attempt to capture an emotional depth with which those experiencing breakdown could identify, and to Helen Denholm, who offered constructive advice and encouragement from the beginning.

I should also like to thank everyone who relived their personal experiences of breaking up for this book so that others might benefit. Their names have been changed, but their stories are real. Sharing these events with such honesty and openness was truly special.

Introduction

The whole subject of the breakdown of relationships is surrounded by an apparently ever-growing cloud of confusion and debate. What is the real impact of a breakdown on the individuals concerned? What are the general implications of increasing rates of relationship breakdown on our culture? How are we supposed to deal with such a breakdown? A single, conclusive answer to each of these questions has yet to be found, probably because the perception of partnership – of what it really means to each of us – has undergone a dramatic transformation over time.

Partnership is usually regarded as being about fulfilling personal expectations, about achieving individual dreams, hopes and ideals. Our expectations of a partnership are different from those of our parents, just as they, in turn, had different expectations from those of their parents. The idea of partnership has generated a host of grey areas in our understanding of the concept, while the *ideal* of partnership has created illusions, fragile assumptions, confusion and frustration.

Today, partnership does not necessarily mean marriage, and an increasing number of couples are choosing to live together rather than marry. Living together is a form of commitment, and when it comes to relationship breakdown, those who have cohabited have invested time, energy and faith in the future of the partnership just as married couples have done. They are likely to have to divide up shared property. They will have shared friends and become involved with their respective 'in-laws'. They will have built a life around the partnership.

Commitment is the basic common denominator of all partnerships, married or not, and this book is, therefore, for anyone who has gone through the breakdown of a partnership. When the word 'marriage' is used, it applies to all partnerships, because in the face

5

of a breakdown we are all equals. The trauma affects each of us as deeply as war, disease or a natural disaster. Wherever you have come from, wherever you are going, breakdown is the great leveller. And it is time we began to try to understand it – and to understand what it can do to us as human beings.

Some aspects of breakdown are universal, but each individual will experience them in his or her own way. This book contains the accounts of a number of relationship breakdowns: you will identify with some of these, but not with others. But if there is one fact, no matter how small, within these pages that makes your journey smoother or that helps you along the way, the book will have served its purpose.

This said, it is worth taking a brief overview of divorce and of what it means. Divorce, on a large scale, is a relatively modern phenomenon, but we have come to accept that it is here to stay. Everyone has at least one friend or relative who has been through a divorce, and in some ways, we tend to regard the breakdown of a marriage as a relatively trivial event – some might say that it is a modern cultural disease. We have learned to live with it and to accept it, and there seems to be a widespread feeling that if someone has been through a breakdown, they should bear the pain bravely, pull themselves together and just get on with life.

There are proponents of the view that divorce is too easy and that the laws pertaining to divorce in the West are too liberal. Strong arguments are put forward to support the idea that people take their marriage vows too lightly because, in divorce, there is always an escape hatch. If the marriage doesn't work out, it doesn't matter. It is easy enough to pack your bags and leave. If a partner leaves you, you simply grieve for a little while and then go out and snare a new partner to fill the gaping hole in your life. This is what many people think – people, that is, apart from those who are either going through it or have been through it.

There are two widely held views about the breakdown of marriage. First, people believe that because divorce is available to anyone who is in a troubled partnership, the decision to separate is nothing more than a short-lived discomfort. In the long term, it is suggested, divorce is a relatively painless option. Divorce is easy. When it is regarded in this light, it seems as if divorce is something like a surgical procedure: if you remove the cause of the ailment – in this instance a marriage – all will be well. True, everything will heal, given the appropriate support and given that the people concerned come to terms with what has happened. In many cases, however, although divorce may be the wisest choice, it is not painless. It takes time to recover from a separation, and we are never the same again.

The second assumption is that the rate and magnitude of divorce is such that it is an experience for which we will naturally have the skills to deal. This assumption is both naïve and potentially damaging to those who are going through a breakdown. Anyone who is experiencing a divorce feels lost and alone. They turn to others for guidance on what they are feeling and how deeply they should be feeling it. They have to come to terms with the end of an era in their lives. Rebuilding and beginning again and having faith in the future take a great deal of courage.

Breakdown is never, ever fluid, simple or easy, and when it happens, those who are going through it are often reduced to the basic functions of emotional survival. The pain, vulnerability and confusion engendered by relationship breakdown can often be psychologically crippling, if only in the short term.

When we are physically hurt we can turn to painkillers, and a doctor who can diagnose the problem and provide treatment so that the pain goes away. With breakdown there are no painkillers. The pain must be lived through, and the degree to which we heal depends on our own desire to recover and the availability of people around us who are willing to offer love and support.

Why is breakdown so deeply traumatic? Because the loss is not confined to the relationship. It is not just about losing a partner. It is about losing things that we are not sure we will ever retrieve – faith, dreams, ideals, security and purpose. In short, we lose the meaning of daily existence. Whether we are aware of it or not, these facets of our lives have become enmeshed in a relationship, and when the relationship falls apart, our self-belief falls apart as well. When the initial shock is over, we begin to wonder how, and if, we will ever put the pieces back together and, even if we do, whether they will fit in the same way. They won't, of course, we know that they won't, and that is where the depth of the pain originates: in the knowledge that life will never be the same again. *We* will never be the same again.

Even though it may be difficult to acknowledge it, this knowledge can be a good thing. If we are willing to work towards self-discovery, it can be rewarding.

When the breakdown first occurs, it can feel as if we are drowning in a wave of emotion. Overwhelmed by grief and fear for the future, it seems impossible to believe that we can pass through the darkness to the other side. There is no one to tell us how, and it is difficult to believe that we will have the strength to try. Comfort can be taken from a simple thing – knowledge. Once we understand that what we are feeling is normal and part of the experience of breaking up, we begin to realize that there is a way out.

This book is about journeying through and out of the emotional devastation that breaking up inflicts on everyone who goes through it. It does not attempt to paper over the cracks of the experience nor does it make light of the emotional impact of breaking up. This is because it is only when the intensity and depth of the impact is acknowledged that it is possible to begin to deal with it. And the more honest we are with ourselves and with those around us about what is happening inside, the sooner and better will we be enabled to heal. To heal and to begin again.

1

Is This Really Happening to Me?

I couldn't believe you could feel as bad as that and not be in hospital. It was physical. I felt physically ill and physically sick a lot of the time. I was in shock in a big way. I couldn't sleep. I couldn't eat. I couldn't anything. I couldn't do anything other than think about what had happened. It was gut-wrenching.

Caroline, aged 41, separated

CAROLINE IS A real person, who was interviewed for this book on the subject of the breakdown of her twenty-year marriage. Her words aptly define the experiences of thousands of others who have been through relationship breakdown.

There is no such thing as an easy divorce or an easy breakdown. Losing a partner is profoundly disturbing, and an experience we must find a way to come to terms with. However, before we can begin to come to terms with relationship breakdown, we must first acknowledge this:

The impact that the loss of a partner will have on our lives cannot be underestimated. Until the breakdown, our partnership fulfilled a most fundamental role in shaping the meaning and structure of our daily existence and our beliefs about the future.

Did any one of us ever believe that a partnership in which we had invested so many of our dreams, so much of our time and the majority of our hopes for the future would end this way? When it happens to us, it brings with it a sense of unreality. We cannot help asking ourselves: 'Is this really happening to me?' What we experience is physical shock, which seems to come from the outside and permeate our whole being. The implications are of a magnitude we can hardly grasp, hence our initial feeling that it is not real. Breakdown also makes us profoundly vulnerable.

At first, we might put down our reaction to the possibility that we take our partnership more seriously than the rest of coupled society does their own. After all, people divorce or split up after living together, spend a few months recovering and then get on with it, don't they? If breakdown is part of modern life, shouldn't we deal with it like modern people with modern solutions? In our society, the number of divorced people runs into the millions, and in some countries, the divorce rate is as high as one in two. Shouldn't we have got used to it by now?

There is one simple answer to each of these questions: 'No.'

Breakdown is a deeply felt personal experience. It can plunge you into a depth of despair of which you didn't imagine yourself capable. Yet it can also be the precursor of a radical and potentially positive and renewing transformation in your character and your life. It affects your self-identity, your ability to relate to others, your sense of self-worth, your ideals and, ultimately, your ability and desire to achieve self-fulfilment. The effects of breakdown should never be underestimated in either the short or long term.

The first few days, weeks and perhaps even months of the breakdown of a relationship can be associated with a sense of unreality and numbness, and, for many, a sense of overwhelming grief. This is normal. Before we go on to explore this, it is most important to point out that if you have only recently experienced the breakdown of a relationship, you must remember that these sensations will pass. You will recover. Hard though it may be to believe when you are in the first devastating throes of the darkest period, you will recover.

Partnership means great expectations

If breakdown has become part of the common fabric of our society, an accepted 'norm', why does it affect each of us so profoundly? There are a multitude of reasons, only a few of which we have the space to explore here.

When we get married, we have great expectations. While most of us are, to varying extents, aware of the increasing divorce rate, we still believe in the sanctity of our own marriage. Other marriages might fail, but not ours. Although we may, rationally, be aware of the risk that our relationship may end in breakdown, we are still imbued with the cultural ideal that 'marriage is for life'. Little do we consider how much has changed since this concept of lifelong partnership was maintained as a realistic goal.

For one thing, our expectations of marriage have changed greatly since the last century. At one time, the decision to marry was based on familial and economic grounds. Now, we look to partnership for emotional fulfilment, to gratify our needs for personal happiness. We look to it for the achievement of our romantic ideals. And, considering the disparity in emotional needs between men and women and, more specifically, the unique aspirations of each individual, we are asking a great deal of the married state.

Second, when we consider the 'marriage is for life' principle, we must remember that 'life' is no longer what it used to be. We can expect to live longer than our parents and our grandparents, and much longer than our not-too-distant ancestors. We are asking for our unique emotional needs to be met by one person for a considerable period of time. And remember this: no one will stagnate within a marriage or partnership. Over time, everyone changes, and our needs and expectations of our partner and our marriage will change, too. We cannot begin to envisage what our personal needs will be ten, twenty or thirty years from now. A 'marriage is for life' rule that is based on the fulfilment of personal expectations, as is the case today, is a tall order.

When we wed, we have great expectations of marital felicity. We make a commitment, and, whether we are conscious of it or not, our partnership becomes the nexus from which the rest of our experience evolves and from which it derives meaning. Partnership becomes the context through which we synthesize and make sense of our lives: our social interaction, our personal development, our goals, our beliefs, our individual identity and even the daily routine of our lives. How quickly we forget that we once lived and even thrived as a single individual. We are now someone's 'other half', and we allow ourselves to drift into the misconception that our relationship with our partner exists outside ourselves as an entity in its own right. Eventually, we come to regard the partnership as sustaining us. It becomes our reason for being, and without it, we are nothing.

The corollary of this view is that, if the partnership is an entity on its own, it should be able to survive in isolation from ourselves. How many times have you heard yourself talk about 'your marriage' as if it were an object you procured at the register office or church? Perhaps you are even now thinking to yourself that 'your marriage failed', but you find the idea inconceivable. After all, you put everything you had into it but it still failed. Therefore, you feel that *you* have failed. Whatever you were able to give wasn't enough to make it survive. This is an important point and one that we will consider in more detail later. For now, however, we need to understand the initial impact of breakdown. Even for those who try to bury the impact, attempting to paper over the cracks of their emotional experiences, there will ultimately be a need to come to terms with loss.

Let us look at the experience of William, a fifty-year-old civil servant who has been divorced once and is now separated from his second wife. William married Lyn in 1967 when he was twenty-one. He believes that, to a certain extent, they both married to 'escape' from their home environments. He saw himself as the dutiful husband, bringing home his wage packet and being a father to their two children. 'To me, it was the sort of marriage that I thought people had. The bloke went to work, did a good job, put the money on the table and looked after the family,' he said.

And all was well – until the ninth year of their marriage, when William discovered that Lyn was having an affair. Breaking up the marriage was too horrible to contemplate, and he waited the better part of a year in the hope that it was a passing thing. But it wasn't. The marriage broke up and Lyn moved in with the other man. William could not understand why. He had done all the things a husband should.

'It was so painful. It just seems as if everything I had lived for and hoped for ... all the dreams had gone. At the time it was just, "why?" With a strict Catholic upbringing, you think you only have one chance ... and I'd blown it. So it wasn't just my wife I had lost, it was myself. Then there was all the worry about the future, the children, what would happen to them, what would happen to me. ... All I wanted was to make the pain go away.'

William found a way to make the pain go away by leaping into another relationship with someone he met at work. Jacqueline was the single mother of a young boy, and this offered William the perfect solution. They needed someone to care for them, so the role of partner and father was awaiting him. He had found a bandage for the pain. His divorce came through in 1978, and he married Jacqueline in 1979. They also had two children. However, during the mid- to late 1980s, William began to notice changes in his wife's behaviour. She was becoming more independent, and then, once again, after nearly ten years of marriage, Jacqueline announced that she wanted to leave him.

'It was just as if someone had hit me over the top of the head with a hammer and the shock wave went right down ... I remember I was at the top of the stairs and just sort of standing there. It was physical. I actually felt from the top of my head a waverunning right down through my feet and there was terror at the tail end of it. "It's happened again. What am I going to do?" I was a family man and a good guy and here it happened to me a second time.'

As a marriage evolves, we come to depend on it. We become part of it and immersed in it. In the early days, when we embark on a marriage, we have personal, idealistic expectations of our union – expectations not just of our partner, but of the marriage itself. These expectations are different for each individual, and we are not usually even aware of the standards by which we judge our own happiness. We tend to become painfully aware of them only when they are not being met. Getting married, or perhaps more accurately, becoming married, has a lot to do with ideals, illusions and self-image. What will my marriage do for me? If I contribute this and that, I can expect that it will give this in return. I don't have to explore these expectations to any depth, because, if I am married, the rest will naturally follow.

The emotional bombshell

When a relationship breaks down, the shock we experience is our way of protecting ourselves from the grim reality of what is happening to us. For several reasons the initial realization of the impending breakdown is too much for us to take in and accept. Whether you have initiated the breakdown or whether you are the one who has been left, the split is going to have tremendous effects on your life: you are not just losing a partner, you are losing an entire lifestyle.

When we set up house in a marriage or partnership, we create a fabric of existence that is built on and around the expectation of sharing our life with another. We 'build' a life together. Each day is a new brick, cemented to the structure that is our partnered life by shared experiences and aims. Over time, the structure grows, as children, new friends and relations, changes in lifestyle, shared moments and experiences are brought to it – everything, in fact, that results from the two partners investing their most precious assets – time, energy and faith in the future – in the relationship.

Is it any surprise, therefore, that the effects of breakdown can be so profound? Breaking up is not simply the end of a relationship. The event strikes at the structure and foundation of our lives, undermining our sense of purpose and destroying our inner identity.

Caroline, a forty-one-year-old journalist, had been separated from her husband for a year and was still feeling the impact of her breakdown. She had met her husband when she was sixteen years old, and they were married when she was twenty. Her husband, Tom, who was twenty-three when they married, worked in the building trade.

'Right from the word go,' Caroline said, 'from day one, the most noticeable thing about us was that we got on incredibly well. I always felt we were best friends as well as husband and wife, and this lasted throughout the marriage until the breakdown. Everybody thought we were the ideal couple. They would say, "Oh, you and Tom get on so well together ... you are always doing things together." '

Tom, who had lost his father when he was a child, bonded closely with Caroline's parents. Caroline was an only child and, almost immediately, her family was extended by the inclusion of Tom. Her father became Tom's substitute father, and Tom was the 'son he never had'. Caroline and Tom delayed having their own children until she was twenty-seven. Consequently, they had what

Caroline describes as a 'carefree life', with a rich social life and a wide network of friends.

After nearly twenty years of marriage, the bombshell exploded and reduced the structure of Caroline's life to emotional rubble – in 1995 the marriage ended amid a period of family tribulations. Tom's business had gone into liquidation. By then, they had two girls, Rosie, who was thirteen, and Andrea, who was nine. Yet although the family had been through a rough patch financially and emotionally, Caroline had just got a new full-time job and she believed the future was looking much brighter. She felt that, at last, things were beginning to look up and that it was time she and Tom sat down and cleared the air so that they could plan for the future.

So, full of enthusiasm and prepared for a fresh start, she broached the issue when they had both arrived home from work one February evening. But Tom did not want to talk about the future. Caroline wanted to know why. 'Can't you guess?' he asked. 'I want to leave you.' Caroline refused to accept what was happening. 'It just sort of dawned on me horribly. I felt just sick. Just awful. It definitely wasn't happening to me. I felt like I was in another world, really. I could not believe it. I just felt my whole life had ended, I'd lost everything. I knew I'd got my children and that, but you don't think about the positive things when you are that far down. I thought, "That's it. I've lost the lot." '

She spent the following week battling for her marriage. But Tom was resolute. 'I was just pleading with him, wringing my hands. Everything that he tried to do to convince me otherwise, I just wanted him to stay. I couldn't bear the thought of him leaving. I felt very desperate and would have done anything. If he'd said, "go and lie down in the middle of the road and let a car run over you and I'll stay," I would have done it. I would have literally done anything.'

In retrospect, Caroline realizes that the battle was futile, but she was desperate. She was desperate because she was losing not just her husband; she was losing an entire life. Since she was sixteen years old, she had invested the better part of twenty-five years of her energy, her time and herself in the marriage – it was a living entity on which her sense of security and well-being relied. The marriage had a refined, complex network of nerve endings, which permeated her daily consciousness. These were the result of the evolution of a total synergy between Caroline and Tom, their marriage, family, friends, shared experiences through joys and setbacks, and, finally, through their children. She had faith in the future of the marriage, and she was shocked to realize that it could be so vulnerable and could be ended in a single evening, by one swift and fatal stroke. Even though many ingredients had built up over the years to contribute to the final outcome, the breakdown, Caroline experienced it as a sudden death, as a bereavement.

Breakdown can be worse than bereavement

When someone we love dies, in the majority of cases we know that they have not left us from choice, and that knowledge affords us at least some comfort. If your partner has left you, however, you are expected to cope. Surely, people think, being left is not a fate worse than death! Moreover, if you are the one who has done the leaving, no one expects you to experience any form of loss. After all, it was your decision, your choice, wasn't it?

These common assumptions are far from the truth. The breakdown of a relationship can, in fact, be worse than bereavement. Bereavement offers us cultural rituals to help us deal with our loss. There is a body, a coffin and a funeral service. With breakdown, however, there is nothing physical to represent our loss, nothing for us to kneel before, alongside our relatives. There is no service or ritual at which we can say our prayers, to begin to let go and to transmute our shock into a performance designed to act as a buffer for our pain. At the end of a relationship, something intangible dies – a dream, perhaps, a partnership, certainly – but something that was alive and defined our lives as long as we were part of a couple. Because there is no body for people to see, we are simply expected to cope.

When a relationship breaks down, it is far more difficult to let go because our partner is still walking around. Every time we see him or her, we must relive the pain. In death, we have the death itself, an event beyond our control, as the cause of and 'excuse' for our feelings and our sense of loss. When a relationship ends, we look for something or someone to blame. There is no excuse for our feelings, so we seek to apportion blame, and, inevitably, we will blame either ourselves or our ex-partner. We have to find a way to channel our sense of loss.

If we and others treated relationship breakdown with the same respect and compassion as bereavement, we would be far better able to deal with the loss of our partner.

The common emotional reactions

When people experience a relationship breakdown and experience it profoundly, they often question the normality of what they are feeling and the length of time their experiences may last. What is normal? The simple, but perhaps most frustrating, answer is: whatever you are feeling now. You can go from an emotional 'high', which results from the relief of being released from a miserable marriage, to plunge into dark suicidal thoughts, brought on by a deep sense of loss or failure.

Emotional reactions can begin with shock and extend through anxiety and depression. But what do these words mean? We have all heard them before, but they have become hackneyed and made almost meaningless from repeated use in modern language ever since the advent of psychoanalysis.

To you, these reactions are real and intense, and you may find some relief in knowing that these words can be defined. These are some of the common emotional and physical reactions that you may experience:

- Shock: confusion; difficulty in concentrating or focusing enough to do daily tasks.
- Anger: waves of blame and resentment towards your partner, fuelled by a sense of powerlessness; or anger turned inwards in the form of self-reproach and guilt.
- Anxiety: constant worrying; fear for the future; feeling out of control.
- Depression: feelings of lethargy and fatigue; great sadness; sense of pointlessness.

- Isolation: a tendency to withdraw socially; tiredness; despair.
- Loss of confidence: negative thoughts about one's own self-worth, leading to low self-esteem and a sense of inadequacy.
- Increased activity: anxiety may make you rush into great activity to stop yourself from feeling.
- Insomnia: sleeplessness.

The first step towards acceptance

The first fledgling step we make after a breakdown is to try to understand what has happened. Why did it happen? Why did it happen to me? There is so much to understand and, at the outset, you will feel confused, and it is important to bring your daily life down to the simplest common denominator.

Think about yourself and what you need to do to survive emotionally in the short term.

If you can do that, gradually you will begin to absorb all of the things that have happened to you. You may begin to realize that, to a certain extent at least, you are a victim of the cultural and social expectations about the concept of marriage. Moreover, you should attempt to be kind to yourself and say: 'What I'm feeling, as deeply as I'm feeling it, is ok and normal.' If you can begin to work this through, you will find that these are the first steps towards making sense of, and sifting through, the emotional rubble that lies before you.

The most important thing to do right now is to set up 'markers' – things that will help you comprehend and deal with your experiences. Identify your feelings. If you are confused, accept that you will be confused. If you are despairing, accept that you will be despairing. If you are frightened, accept that this is a natural response to what has happened to you. Know that this is a necessary part of a process – and be aware that it is a process, which means that it will not last for ever and that there naturally follows another stage. Above all, remember that it will pass.

Look for support. Don't be afraid to ask for it from your family and friends. Try to discuss what you are feeling with those with whom you feel comfortable and spend time with them. Although many people feel a genuine wariness of counselling – 'If I need counselling, there really must be something wrong with me!' – it is also a sensible option. If you had any other difficulty or problem, such as a toothache or a concern about your physical health, you would most likely take the common-sense step of seeking the advice and help of an expert. The same can be applied to dealing with one of the most difficult and painful experiences any one of us can have – relationship breakdown. How you are feeling and coping matters!

Think about what you need most and take the first steps towards getting what you need to help you cope with what you are experiencing.

2

When Your Partner Leaves

When she finally left, I said to myself, 'What have I done?' If I had been a womanizer, or spent the mortgage money down at the pub, or gambled it away, I could then say to myself, 'Well, it's your own fault.' It was so deeply frustrating. I didn't know where to put the blame. I couldn't say: 'This is why I have failed.'

Hugh, aged 38, divorced

JUST AS THERE are two sides to every story, there are also two sides to a breakdown – that of the person who has chosen to end it and that of the one who has been left behind. Although sometimes relationship breakdowns are the result of mutual decisions, most often they are the result of a choice made by one of the partners, and for this reason there are two distinct perspectives, two sides of the same coin, of the same shared experience. The partners will experience some common emotional reactions to the breakdown, but for the most part, each will have a dramatically different perspective on the same event.

Let's take a closer look at one side of that coin. Your partner has decided to end it. He or she is gone, and it's as if the ground is crumbling beneath you.

We have heard other people describe their initial experiences of the breakdown of relationships as being characterized by a sense of unreality and by a feeling that they just could not accept what was happening. A common reaction is that it is as if it were happening to somebody else. In the previous chapter we saw how Caroline tried to persuade her husband to stay so that the marriage could be salvaged, while William hoped that his first wife's affair would just go away so that they could carry on as usual. In the end, both

Caroline and William were left by their partners. Yet they both felt they had failed. They both saw the structures that had been their marriages, into which they had put years of effort, disintegrate, leaving them with feelings of shock, devastation and loss, but there was nothing they could do to prevent those feelings. Both were victims of a terrible loss, yet each said: 'What have I done wrong to cause this?' After the shock, we attempt to come to terms with, and to make sense of, what has happened to us by whatever means we can. We ask 'Why did it happen?' and we look for explanations for feelings of hurt and bewilderment, no matter how unrealistic that may be.

After Caroline's husband left, she admits to having 'hung on' for a period of six months, vainly grasping at the hope that he would come back. William attempted to avoid grief and to paper over the cracks of his self-image by immediately finding a new partner. 'If I could get somebody else who was even more attractive than my first wife, so much the better. And I did,' he said.

Nevertheless, both Caroline and William had to face the ultimate psychological effects, the aftermath, of being deserted. Sooner or later, we must deal with what has happened to us, and it is worth pointing out that they – along with many others – did just that very successfully.

The aftermath of breakdown

Most of us will, at some time or other, have seen on television the after-effects of a nuclear bomb. First, there is the impact. Then a black, mushroom-shaped cloud reaches towards the sky. We can see the cloud expanding at a terrific rate, and we know that the contents of the black mushroom are the results of the first shock of impact as the bomb struck the surface. We can barely grasp the magnitude of the effects that this bomb will have on the surrounding environment.

A psychological parallel can be drawn between this and the emotional devastation wrought in our lives when our partner deserts us. First, there is shock. The tremendous release of emotions and thoughts that naturally follows mushrooms out of proportion until they seem to be too complex for us to comprehend or deal with. It is as if everything is out of our control.

What happens to us when our partner decides to end it? Let us examine some of the emotions that the initial impact of the breakdown of a relationship can generate. You may recognize some of the following reactions: a sense of abandonment or desertion; despair; panic; fear; desperation; helplessness; anger (towards ourselves or our partner); hurt; rejection; betrayal; loss; a sense of personal worthlessness; and, ultimately, a sense of personal failure.

When you consider the range of potential reactions, it will come as no surprise to know that suicidal thoughts are also common. Many of the people who have shared their experiences of breakdown for the purposes of this book admitted to having these thoughts, and some of them went so far as to attempt suicide. At the time, it seemed as if this was the only escape from what was happening. But they realize now that this is not the answer. There are other ways out of the darkness.

If you are feeling so low that suicide seems to be the only option, please do something about it. Get some help. There are people who are available to listen and to understand. Be fair to yourself. You cannot stop loving your partner overnight, and losing a partner and a partnered lifestyle is like losing a vital part of yourself. It will take time and effort to heal.

Your self-esteem: a casualty of breakdown

Among the most crippling effects of being deserted by your partner is a loss of self-esteem, a loss that is as deep-seated as it is far-reaching. The effects begin at the core of your being and extend painfully into your immediate family and through to the outer perimeter of your social environment, only to rebound and return to you in a different form. You will need to be able to deal with it. We will examine the effects of any social stigma that may arise from your loss of feelings of self-worth in a later chapter, but for the moment we will concentrate on loss of self-esteem in terms of the immediate impact of losing your partner.

There appear to be some differences in how this loss of self-esteem is dealt with by the sexes, and it seems to have a lot to do with gender expectations of what needs to be achieved to maintain self-esteem. There are also generational differences. The attitudes of divorcing couples in their thirties, when both partners are more likely to have established careers, are bound to differ somewhat from those in their late forties, fifties or sixties.

For women who are in their forties or older, the experience can have additional far-reaching and devastating implications. Many feel that they have given 'the best years of their lives' to the marriage, and when their husband or partner leaves, they feel cast off, unattractive and worthless − 'past their sell-by date' as the current cliché has it. In many cases, they have given up their personal development to remain at home and fulfil the roles of wife and mother. Over the years they have provided emotional and domestic support to the husband while he built his career. This support has been their investment in the marriage, and a marriage of ten, twenty or thirty years or more is a considerable investment. Add to this the fact that often they do not have the necessary skills or professional training to enable them to support themselves or their children in financial terms after their partner has left.

Is it not understandable that a woman is these circumstances might feel of little worth to herself or to society? Being deserted by her partner implies that she has failed by the standards that have hitherto governed her sense of self-worth. Immediately following the breakdown, she has no other guidelines against which she can assess herself.

Emotional experiences of desertion or abandonment are bound to make us feel rejected and worthless in the short term. We need to redefine the parameters by which we put a value on our own self-worth. We need to revisit the concepts of 'good wife and mother' or, for that matter, of 'faithful husband and provider'. We must embark on a path of self-discovery that starts at the beginning in order to find who we really are and what we can realistically expect from ourselves. There are many more psychological frameworks than marriage through which we can generate feelings of self-worth, but we need to learn what they are.

For men of the baby-boom generation in particular the breakdown of a relationship seems to reflect on their ability to 'hang on to a partner'. Somehow it seems especially shameful to them to be deserted. It is a deflating, confusing process for which they would like to find an immediate cure. Of course, not all men will react in the same way, but they often find it difficult to identify or express what they are feeling, and they may not receive much in the way of encouragement from their peers. They might feel under pressure, either from their own need not to show weakness or from their environment, to keep a stiff upper lip and to maintain their image, and thereby their self-esteem.

When William's second wife left him and he felt deserted yet again, he resorted once more to a tactic that had worked the first time: he looked for an 'aspirin' or a 'bandage', another partner – and fast. He came from what he describes as a 'macho environment in the west of Scotland' and felt that, when he was abandoned, he needed to prove to his peers that there was nothing wrong with him.

'I was so desperate. I think now, what I was really fighting against was losing my self-esteem,' he said. 'Almost straight away, it was as if I had built-in radar. Every time I heard a pair of high heels, my head turned. I thought to myself, "Oh, there's somebody else" ... and "Oh, look, there's somebody else ... they look ok." Again, I was looking for my aspirin. Before I knew it, I was back in a new partner-type relationship. Looking back, I can see that I had a great need for somebody to be there to show I was ok. A driving need that, at the end of the day, was really a lack of awareness of my own worth.'

But William's 'aspirin' didn't work this time. He couldn't paper over the cracks any longer. He described what happened afterwards as being like the bursting of an emotional dam, the crumbling of a psychological barrier. However, this turned out to be the first step towards regaining himself and discovering his own sense of self-worth.

Breakdown and short-lived marriages

The breakdown of marriages of a shorter duration, of less than ten years, does not necessarily mean that the impact on our sense of self-esteem is any the less. We experience an acute sense of failure, perhaps the more so for not being capable of 'making it last'. It raises uncomfortable feelings, such as: 'What, over so fast? Did you even make a proper go of it? You made a supposed lifelong commitment and you couldn't even make it past the starting gate. You must be so inadequate that your partner couldn't bear to stay around long enough to share the joy of the children's first steps, or their first day at school.'

Self-punishing thoughts are common in breakdown, no matter how long the relationship lasted. They are a result of our painful attempts to work out blame. Whatever the length of the partnership, you entered into it with the expectations of dream-fulfilment.

Hugh, a thirty-eight-year-old structural engineer, is a good example. He and his former wife, Annie, met at work when she was doing some temporary work for his company in 1986. They went out to lunch often with other colleagues, and Hugh had time to get to know her. After her temporary contract ended and she had left, Hugh began to date Annie. Eventually, they moved in together and had a warm, happy relationship. 'It was sort of Mills & Boon stuff,' Hugh recalls. 'I thought, "This is the one for me," as they say.'

They lived together for about two years before wedding plans were in the offing. There was no proposal of marriage, but Hugh said that it seemed the natural progression of their relationship, and an expensive, fairytale wedding followed in September 1989. They were both thirty-three years old at the time. Almost immediately after the marriage, Annie began having some emotional problems, and she went to see a counsellor. Her problems had a lot to do with her upbringing, as Hugh was to discover. Annie's mother had died when she was thirteen, and her father had been an alcoholic and physically abusive.

Hugh sees himself as a placid, easy-going person. He tried to be patient, but Annie refused to discuss her counselling sessions and became more and more distant. By the spring of 1990, less than a year after the wedding, she moved out of the master bedroom without explanation. Over the coming months, she refused to stay in the same room with him, then in the same house. In the summer, she left him without stating a reason and without offering a forwarding address. Hugh felt a terrible sense of failure. Yet he had set himself a terrible task.

'I thought perhaps I could make things better for her ... to try and take the pain and suffering she'd had in her younger life and make it better. I had got the sticking plaster that would hide thirty years of pain, suffering and mistrust. It was an impossible task. I realize that now. Once you step back from the situation, you realize that it was impossible to do. But my self-esteem went right down. She moved out in June or July, I think. I was very shaken after that. I know that each day was a survival course.'

Whatever the length of the partnership, we place the onus for our self-esteem on the fate of the marriage, and in so doing we externalize our method of valuing ourselves. When the partnership crumbles, so does our self-esteem. In perceiving and valuing our own self-worth through the looking-glass of our marriage, we are not taking responsibility for ourselves. We make ourselves both vulnerable and victim to the potential failure of an entity, the partnership, that exists outside ourselves. When we reclaim responsibility for the standards by which we value ourselves and for the ways in which we define those standards, we are able, in essence, to reclaim ourselves.

Loss of control and helplessness

When we are left by our partner, we lose not only the relationship but also a sense of control over our environment and what happens to us within it. We are as much victims of loss as anyone who has lost a loved one in a fatal accident. The loss happened *to* us. We feel helpless and powerless, and, once again, the question looms: 'Why?' A sense of loss of control and helplessness can often lead to anxiety or panic attacks and fear for the future. It can also lead to depression and lethargy.

When we feel helpless, we also feel there is little we can do to establish order in our lives. We are like driftwood borne on the powerful waves of chance or the whims of others. The tiniest task can seem to require an act of will. We feel weak and shaken because the commitment in which we had such faith, our marriage, has disintegrated and there was nothing we could do to turn the tide of our personal affairs.

When Annie left Hugh, even though he had tried so hard to get to the root of their problems and failed, after he watched her walk out of the door, he realized that she would never come back. He felt he had lost control over his own life. He said: 'I'd wake up in the morning totally drained. Getting to work was a major achievement. Doing a day's work was an effort. You can con yourself to a certain extent, but then reality strikes you and you realize that you are *not* coping. All you are doing is just surviving. I felt I was walking on a tightrope and there was "life" at the end wiggling the rope. I was close to going over the edge. Close to falling off the rope. I had no control.'

The summer Annie left, Hugh had an opportunity for promotion at the company for which he worked. He failed the promotion board examination, and he thought that part of the reason was his confused mental and emotional state. Realizing he was not coping, Hugh sought out counselling, and it was then he first began to put the pieces back together. He learned to stop asking the questions, 'Why?' 'What did I do wrong?' Instead, he learned to focus on his own needs and to set himself small goals to begin with. For example, he set goals such as making sure that he had a clean, ironed shirt to put on every morning before work or that he cooked himself a proper meal in the evening – things that may be normal everyday tasks for most people but that, for Hugh, seemed like scaling Mount Everest simply because he felt he had no control.

By setting ourselves reasonable goals and by focusing on our own needs, we can re-establish a sense of control over our lives.

Who's to blame?

The most destructive aspect of our quest to understand our current painful circumstances is, ultimately, attempting to apportion blame. The concept of blame is as inherently negative as is its application. When we blame ourselves or blame another, we are selecting a focus for our pain, anger and rejection. It is merely a return to the old question, 'Why?' – 'Why did she leave me?' 'What did I do wrong?' 'It's all his fault. I gave him the best of myself, of my life, everything I had, and he simply destroyed our family by walking away. Why?'

Laying the blame at the door of the partner who has deserted us gives our anger an opportunity for a thorough work-out, but the anger can fester inside and gradually ferment into bitterness. We say to our friends and our family: 'Look what my partner did to me. Isn't he or she a nasty person?' And everybody will agree: your partner is, indeed, a nasty person for rejecting you.

What leads to loss of self-esteem is not only a sense of failure, but a sense of rejection. When we are rejected by our partner for another person, feelings of hurt, betrayal and anger can run deep. The awareness of betrayal can deliver an intense pain, and our reaction is a powerful desire to lash out and to achieve retribution. But who are we really hurting in the long run?

People are capable of hanging on to bitterness about an ex-partner for years, until long after that partner has gone off and created a new life for themselves. The bitterness is a soul-destroying poison that prevents you from living your life to the full. Examine your bitterness and count the number of pleasurable moments it has given you. Ask yourself how much it contributes to your current quality of life and your ability to move forward within it. We will examine in more detail feelings of anger and how they can sometimes help you get through the initial period following breakdown, but if you allow those feelings to ferment for too long, anger will turn to bitterness as surely as wine turns to vinegar.

You are likely to immerse yourself in a post-mortem, trying to work out why your partner left you. You will most probably look at who's to blame. It is a need we each have in us to make sense of the rejection, the loss and the pain.

If only I had acted differently …

Blaming ourselves, however, is the equivalent of taking a large stick and repeatedly beating ourselves over the head with it. Self-blame eats away at our self-esteem. We say things to ourselves, like: 'I am a worthless person. Even my husband or wife thought so little of me that he or she had to leave.' Without self-esteem, we become immobilized. We do not have the courage or the confidence to find out what the future holds in store for us. But what is the purpose of hurting ourselves?

Eight years into their marriage Tom and Caroline experienced a period of setbacks, one of which became a 'timebomb' that exploded twelve years later. It became a weak link in the chain of trust. In 1984 Tom's construction company was crumbling, and he was forced to liquidate his business. At the same time, he began an affair with the sister of one of Caroline's closest friends. Rosie, their first child, was then only eighteen months old.

When Caroline discovered the affair she felt deeply rejected and betrayed. 'I was just desperate to keep the marriage together. I didn't want anybody to know it had happened. I was ashamed that he had gone to somebody else. We were the perfect couple. My confidence just went, my self-esteem just plummeted,' she said. The marriage was patched up, and Caroline promised never to mention Tom's adultery again. They didn't discuss it with anyone or seek help. Twelve years later, she realized that this was a mistake.

In 1995 Tom's second business was going into liquidation. In the previous five years, both of Caroline's parents had died, as had Tom's mother. The familial 'cement' had gone out of their relationship, and they were drifting apart. Tom had been having another affair for a period of six months, and this time he chose to leave. Caroline felt the old rejection awaken with the new. 'It sort of came back with a vengeance. It was history repeating itself.' Her self-esteem plummeted again. She thought he was leaving because the woman with whom he was having the affair was younger and prettier. She thought it was a physical thing. She asked him over and over again, 'What's wrong with me?'

Somehow, somewhere, someone had to be at fault. Caroline was desperately seeking faults in her own person, her appearance, her actions to explain Tom's behaviour.

The worse form of self-blame is to think: 'If only I had done something differently, it might have worked out.' This is an endless treadmill. We continually look for times when a word or a gesture might have turned the tide of the partnership and perhaps prevented the tragedy – 'If I had done such and such on that day, he or she might have stayed. I could have saved my marriage.'

For a long time, Caroline worked out on the 'If only' treadmill. 'I still do,' she said, 'but I don't punish myself with it the way I used to. I'd think things like, "If only we'd talked more. If only

I had taken more notice of what was happening with his business. If only we'd got some counselling after the first affair instead of burying it under the carpet …".'

If only. No matter how many 'If only's' there are, no matter how many scenarios we re-create in our minds, we are still left with the same answer each time. The painful, empty echo of our own thoughts – our own self-blame.

Finding a way out of the darkness

At first, the magnitude and depth of your emotions will seem larger than life, and the cloud containing all the pain of rejection, blame, despair, anger and hurt will appear all-engulfing, but you can and will deal with it. Try to focus on yourself instead of on the partner who has left you. On a day-to-day basis set yourself small tasks that you know you can cope with. Prioritize your activities.

Taking exercise can help to alleviate some of the depression. If you aren't feeling up to vigorous activity, walking for a short distance once or twice a day is a gentle way of getting started and it will give you an opportunity to work through some of your feelings privately. If there are any nearby, quiet places, including parks, walking in areas with trees, rivers or ponds can be soothing.

To begin with, simply be aware each time you are getting on to the 'If only' treadmill and learn to recognize the feelings of inadequacy it generates. In time, practise turning your thoughts away from it.

Surround yourself as much as possible with people who love you. Encourage warm embraces and words of affection from friends and family. Tell them what you need. It will do a lot to ease the pain of rejection and remind you that you are valued and are loved.

If you are really despairing, once again, seek counselling. There are also divorce recovery groups in the UK and United States, where you can share your feelings with others going through the same experiences.

Once you have established a simple daily routine, try to stick to it. Also, learn to accept that you will have bad days, too. Over the coming weeks and months, you will discover that the good days come more often than they used to and the bad days occur less often. Focus on the present. Forge ahead through each day. Repeat to yourself as often as you can that there will be light at the end of the tunnel and that the future holds the promise of change.

3

When You Have Chosen to Leave

I was being torn in all different directions. Everybody wanted a piece of me, to own me. I was destroying their lives. But I had to go. I had done everything I could. I was down to the last little kernel of myself in my heart that no one was going to get. That was all I had left. The rest was gone. If I'd stayed, I would have died.

Sara, aged 49, divorced

ONE OF THE most common, simplistic and tempting assumptions anyone can make about the end of a relationship is that the person who has been deserted is the sole victim of the breakdown.

When someone we know has been left, the lion's share of our attention and sympathy focuses on them. They are the victim, after all, and the decision of the other partner to leave was cruel, uncaring and selfish, and completely devastating to the one left behind.

Most of us will feel genuine sympathy when we hear a friend or family member say: 'My husband left me for another woman after twenty years of marriage', or 'My wife walked out on me without an explanation.' The one left behind is suffering real devastation, loss and anguish, and this person deserves our empathy and our understanding. We are right to care and give our support, for he or she is a victim of the breakdown of the partnership and is suffering loss and grief.

Yet, more often than not, the partner who has chosen to leave is also suffering these emotions.

Let's look at a popular myth. If you have left your partner, you must be in a fairly confident and balanced frame of mind, and you must know what you are doing. You couldn't feel hurt, angry, depressed or grieving, could you? After all, you were the one who decided to end it, and you will have had your reasons. Your mind is made up and you are just going to get on with it. It's a straight-forward task to turn your back on a partnership in which you, also, have invested your time, energy and faith in the future. It's time to move on to greener pastures, so there is no problem and no pain. Does this make sense? No, it does not. It is vital that we examine the other side of the two-sided coin of breakdown that we mentioned in Chapter 2. It is important to understand the true nature of the other side, the side of the person who leaves.

The need to escape

When a person takes the decision to end a partnership, it is usually the result of a long-term build-up of pressures imposed by the marriage, which he or she is no longer able to withstand. Whether the pressures arise because the relationship is unable to accommo-date the growth and change of one or both individuals, whether they emerge from lack of communication or whether they are the consequence of an abusive relationship, the fundamental reason for the pressures is the same, and, regardless of the nature of the pressures, the outcome is the same: the partnership has become dysfunctional. If attempts to rebuild or repair it do not work, we become helpless and defeated within that partnership.

From this sense of helplessness eventually emerges an instinc-tive need to escape, by whatever means. We have all heard stories of how a wild animal will chew off its own leg to escape from a trap in which it has become ensnared. This is truly remarkable, and there is a powerful irony at work here because, by the act of saving itself, the animal becomes a casualty. Yet the agony of self-extrication and permanent injury are preferable to imprison-ment. A parallel can be drawn between this and human rela-tionships, and anyone who has ended a marriage as an act of self-preservation will understand it.

Sooner or later, whatever the means of our escape, no matter how long or how far we have run, even if it is into the arms of another, we must deal with the psychological impact of what we have done and what has led us to do it. We end a partnership when we perceive that we can no longer exist within its confines. We recognize that the structure of the marriage is giving way under pressure. Its inner mechanics are sputtering and groaning under the demands being made of them. But we do not arrive at this perception overnight. We ask ourselves question after question. Is the partnership fatally damaged or can it be repaired?

We can delay making a decision for years by asking ourselves such questions over and over again. It is a terrible and agonizing decision to make. Do I tear down the partnership or try to rebuild it? We are so confused and frightened by having to make a decision because the structure and mechanics of the partnership seem to be inextricably linked. It has defined who we are, and only when the structure is caving in around us, only when the mechanics appear to be grinding to a halt and only when we are overwhelmed by the seemingly insurmountable tasks of repairing and rebuilding do we accept that we have to leave it behind if we are to survive.

When leaving is a last resort

Cases of leaving a partner because of cruelty, selfishness or vindictiveness are rare. More often, whether consciously or subconsciously, the decision to end a partnership is a last resort, and it is on the many who left as a last resort that we will focus our attention.

Fifty-six-year-old Robert, who is now retired from broadcasting, understands the 'last resort' very well. On 5 October 1992 he left his wife Susan after nearly ten years of marriage. He still loved her deeply. He had first met her during a publicity tour of the UK for a friend's book. He was totally smitten with her, and they wrote to each other for several months. They married within a month of Robert's moving house in order to be close to her. 'Both of us knew it was inevitable that we would get married. And we were married on 29 July 1983 ... it was a glorious Friday,' he remembers.

It was on the first few days of their honeymoon that Robert began to realize that something was terribly wrong. An incident at their hotel began to make apparent something that had not been clear before – the depth of Susan's religious commitment. 'We arrived at the hotel for our honeymoon and she was asking the receptionist if there was a "meeting" on in the local area. I had no knowledge what these meetings were,' he said. Robert had known before they got married that Susan attended church regularly, but he said, 'I certainly at the time had no knowledge that she had a complete obsession with religion.'

When they returned home, Robert noticed that the number of Christian meetings that Susan attended increased. Within the first few weeks he began to question her priorities. Which did she put first, the marriage or her God? He felt that Susan treated his questions and his arguments as attacks on her faith. 'I handled the situation very badly. I had had experience beforehand of people being involved in this sort of thing, but not in a close personal relationship. I felt as though I was in a very dark room with not a chink of light.'

Over a period of nine years Susan's religion was a growing bone of contention between them. Robert felt that they both tried hard to make it work, that they both loved each other, but her faith created an unbridgeable divide between them. During the last twelve months of their marriage, he recalls, Susan was out to a 'meeting' every night of the week and twice on Sundays. 'I think two of the things which really stick out in my mind are a complete loss of sense of humour and a realization that I didn't really know what loneliness was like until I got married,' he said.

For Robert, the situation reached crisis point in the summer of 1991: 'I knew that our problems were very deep-seated problems of a religious, political and personal nature. I tried getting angry. That didn't work. I tried pleading. That didn't work. I tried conversation. Nothing actually worked. I realized the futility of it all. The problem was inescapable. It was like being in a very dark, convoluted tunnel and knowing I couldn't walk backwards because the door had been closed and I couldn't see any way in which to walk forwards except to end my life.'

So, while Susan was away on holiday, Robert sat down with a bottle of whisky and used the whole of it to wash down one hundred paracetamol. At the time, he felt that walking away from the marriage wasn't an option. He couldn't face tearing it down, but he realized that he could not repair or rebuild it.

But the story doesn't end there. In fact, that is where it begins. Robert lived and went on to transform his painful experiences into a new way of life, deciding, more than a year after the suicide attempt, that it was necessary to end the relationship. For Robert, the decision to leave was the last resort. He had to end the marriage because the faults in the partnership had grown out of all proportion and he knew that they could not be fixed. The partnership existed as an entity, and he was trapped within it. Robert and Susan's marriage was the entity that structured Robert's life. He could not imagine himself or his life outside it, even when living within that structure became intolerable.

People are not 'weak' because they end a marriage. Often, leaving is an act of strength and of self-preservation. Many people experience futility and helplessness, compounded by a desire to escape from what they see as inescapable. These feelings and emotions affect our perceptions, our daily life and our inner sense of self, and it seems as if we are inseparable from them.

Ending one's life is often contemplated as one avenue of escape, but only because it is impossible to see that there is a future waiting for us outside of the partnership. But there always is a future, and a future that is new, unique and filled with a multitude of new experiences and opportunities – a future, moreover, that is defined by ourselves, our needs and our goals and not by the emotionally disabling effects of a marriage in which we find ourselves deeply miserable, a marriage that has drained us of our sense of self and has, at length, become the reason for our oppression.

When someone else is a means of escape

A means of escape can offer itself in many different forms. It may come in the form of an affair with another person, and this provides us with a tangible purpose in our decision and a focus for the outcome of the pressures we are experiencing. An affair provides the mental and emotional impetus to escape, although this is not to say that the new relationship isn't real, important or genuine.

It is, however, the dysfunctional partnership that leaves us open and receptive to the affair in the first instance. Nothing is ever as simple or as black and white as we might like it to be. Few of us will get married with the intention of being unfaithful, but later, something within or about the marriage will create a predisposition for infidelity or an openness to it. Our great expectations of our partnership are not being met, and either through a desire to fulfil unmet needs, or as a means of giving vent to anger and frustration, or simply as an emotional 'exit visa' we are susceptible to other relationships when the marriage isn't doing what we had expected it to do.

Sara, an only child, was married when she was twenty-two. A significant factor played a decisive role in her choice of partner: her mother had died suddenly when Sara was a teenager, and for many years she was responsible for managing the household for her father. She had always felt she had been robbed of her childhood. Sara met George, her future husband, at a weekend dinner dance where he almost literally swept her off her feet. George, who was twenty-seven at the time, had been divorced from his first wife for only five months, another significant factor that was to affect the marriage.

'He was so attentive and gregarious,' said Sara. 'He came up to visit me for my birthday, bought me an orchid and we stayed in an expensive hotel. All the romantic things. He gave me my first orgasm and I thought that it had to be love.' George proposed to Sara in February 1969, six months after they had first met. 'He got down on his knees and asked me to marry him. He said he wanted to take care of me. I felt as if I could grab back some of the childhood I had lost.'

George had explained to Sara that his first wife had left him for another man. He had been a victim. Consequently, Sara felt that the onus for making the marriage successful was on her shoulders. 'Because George's first wife had left him, I promised myself to make this marriage work.' For the first six months, they were 'ecstatically happy' and 'behaved like children', attending dances and enjoying themselves. It was Sara who suggested that they slow down and begin to behave more responsibly. And it was when they 'slowed down' that Sara was to make a discovery which altered the nature of the marriage for good. George was a manic depressive.

'I only knew him for six months before we were married and then he was in a manic phase – he had the wedding to look forward to. It seemed to me that everything was fine and then the bottom fell out. He was forced to slow down for the first time since his first wife had left and the impact of his breakdown hit him. There was my husband who had promised to take care of me lying on the sofa in his bathrobe and trying to disappear into the crack at the back of it. It was as if a bomb had come down.'

It was the first of many depressive episodes that Sara would face during the next eight and a half years. She felt that she had to take control. She had vowed to make the marriage work, but the honeymoon was over and by the end of the first year of her marriage, Sara was having her first affair. Why? She was angry and hurt. All her great expectations for the marriage had been dashed almost immediately, and she was left with the task of 'making it work'.

'I felt betrayed,' she said. 'He'd come along, the knight on the white charger and said, "I will take care of you." I had left all of my friends, my job and my previous life behind in the town I had been living in to move to the city with him. He had no concept of what I had given up.' Yet she could not leave him, and the pressure began to build. Sara reacted to the pressure by quietly having an affair with an ex-lover in order to give vent to her anger and her frustration.

She spent the following years attempting to please George, yielding to his wishes, hoping that she could find a way to end his depression, to make him happy and to make the relationship work. 'It was the "if ... then" theory,' said Sara. 'I spent eight and a half years thinking, "If I do this, then that will happen and everything will be all right." Every month I thought, "Next month will be better."' George wanted a baby, and Sara complied by trying to get pregnant. But she could not, and after many different kinds of treatment, some of them quite dangerous, had failed, they had to accept that Sara was infertile.

'This eroded my self-esteem more than anything else that had happened in my life. Because my husband had always had every-thing in life he wanted, and here was I who could not give him the one thing he wanted. And, because I had a medical problem, it was my fault. He wanted a baby, so I thought, "Ok, I'll give you a baby." And then, I couldn't. What a failure.'

They adopted a baby girl two years into the marriage. Sara's affair ended, and she stayed at home to look after the child. She thought their prayers had been answered and that everything was going to be all right. But it wasn't. She had still failed to please her husband, who wanted more children. So she agreed that they would become foster-parents, and the house was filled with children. Sara felt lost within it. Gradually, she became withdrawn. Before she had married George, Sara had been an outgoing person, but by 1975 she had taken to 'hiding in the kitchen'. She said: 'I had built a wall around me that was ten feet high and two feet thick. Before I got married, I was a sparkling being. Then I got beaten down day by day, by events, by his attitude. I was the picture of my ageing aunts. Mundane. Middle-aged. At thirty, I was very, very old.'

Sara was reaching breaking point. By February 1977 her second affair had started, but this time it was different. She was approached by a younger man who lived in the neighbourhood. He began to 'drag her out of the kitchen', encouraging her to participate and to join in local activities. 'Somebody saw me as me, rather than as "George's wife". It was frightening. Very frightening. I felt like Dracula being dragged into the sunlight. And I felt I couldn't function out there. But in the end, it was that affair that extricated me from the marriage.'

Eight months later, after marital counselling had failed, Sara finally told George about the two affairs, rented herself a room and left him. It was the beginning of the road to recovery.

Guilt and failure: the price of freedom

No one leaves a marriage without experiencing doubts, fears or feelings of self-blame, but anyone who has left a relationship also knows that to admit openly to such confusion and uncertainty would signal a return to square one. It would mean giving in to pressure to remain within the partnership, and it would mean returning to the place in their consciousness where they know they cannot live – within the partnership.

Being forced to remain in a partnership because of guilt can be harmful to both partners. Sara was constantly reminded by George that it was her responsibility to 'make it work'. She retaliated by fulfilling his worst nightmare – having an affair – and by the time she left, she felt neither respect nor love for him, only the need to retain what was left of her sense of identity and to try to rehabilitate herself and to replace all that she had lost. The second affair provided her with the means to escape and to preserve what was left. However, in escaping the trap, she injured herself with the torturing burden of guilt, a guilt that was laced with an overpowering sense of failure.

After all, she was the one who had left. She felt she had destroyed the lives of her husband and of their daughter and foster-children. Her self-esteem reached rock-bottom, and even after she had left, she berated herself for not having made a success of the marriage. All that she had given had not been enough. 'Three weeks after I left him, I was on my way to attend an aunt's wedding anniversary party. It was a two-hour journey and I cried all the way there. I felt so awful. So worthless. So absolutely worthless. In the photographs of the party, I am nowhere to be seen. I kept hiding. I felt I was so bad that I should be invisible. No one should see me.'

A sense of failure can be pervasive. Robert had tried repeatedly but unsuccessfully to repair his marriage. Although he did not feel as personally responsible as Sara did, he was equally affected by a sense of failure. He did not wish to put Susan out of the marital home and went on the homeless list for three months before a place was found. 'I went to see the resettlement officer and I just burst into floods of tears. I couldn't articulate. I couldn't think straight. I just bit my tongue.... What I recognized was that both of us had simply not been able to make it. It was a sense of infinite sadness. This recognition that two people who'd fallen in love with one another ... had got to this point of total destruction.'

When you take the decision to leave or to end it – when you assume the responsibility for making the choice, even if it is only in order that you might survive – you become vulnerable to feelings of guilt, self-blame and failure. If the partnership has been the means of your oppression, there will, at first, be a sense of euphoria in your new-found freedom. The initial feeling of release can be tremendous, but the dark reminders of guilt and failure will come crowding in. Even then there is more: there is the frightening prospect of standing alone while bearing the burden of your decision.

After the euphoria had faded, Sara recalled: 'I was living alone, totally alone, for the first time in my life. I remember feeling very lost, wondering, "Who am I? What am I?" My life had revolved around doing for others. I had been someone's mother or foster-mother, George's wife, making meals, cleaning.... Taking that out of the equation, I was left with me. I was frightened of being alone.'

Why is it so belittling, so daunting and so soul-destroying to leave a marriage? Part of the reason is that the entity of marriage is bound up with the trappings of morality. We are not so progressive that we can end a marriage without being forced to deal with this as a reality. Being the decision-maker will place you in the unenviable position of bearing the brunt of any criticism that is levelled by those who regard a breakdown in a relationship as a moral failure. In addition, the role of decision-maker is a lonely one and one that few will thank or commend you for taking on.

But here is a truth that cannot be overlooked: leaving is a courageous act. Never forget that you have taken the step against the tide of the demands and expectations of others, that you have done this despite the 'married for life' rule that, although unrealistic, still whispers darkly within the consciousness that to leave is to fail, and that, no matter how harshly others judge you, you are likely to punish yourself more than the rest combined. Think of these things and remind yourself that leaving is a brave thing to do. There will come a time when you will accept this and be able to thank yourself. You did not take the decision to hurt others: you did it as the first step to reclaiming yourself and to reclaiming your life.

Self-forgiveness and acceptance

When two partners experience breakdown, there is a need for both to understand why and to find someone or something to blame. We naturally attach blame to one or other of the partners. We do not consider looking at the marriage in which we are living, at the entity that we created together. Blaming an individual is a futile exercise. Think again about the two-sided coin and you will appreciate that no one can apportion blame to one person simply because it is the synergy of the relationship itself that influences each partner's individual actions.

In the breakdown of a relationship, everyone suffers. For the one who has ended it, the suffering and the pressure have often been building up for years prior to the breakdown. If we can get to grips with and understand this fact, we will recognize that we deserve our own forgiveness and that no fault can be found in acting on the imperative of self-preservation. We wound ourselves with feelings of guilt and failure in order to be free, but the pain is inflicted so that we may survive and we are prepared to pay a price to achieve freedom. There is no sense in continuing to exist on a daily diet of misery while we have the power to free ourselves, and in so doing, we may, when we have healed, have more to give ourselves and others.

What can you do to begin to heal? If you are to deal with self-blame, a sense of worthlessness, isolation and loss you need to learn to live alone. If an affair has been your means of extrication from a relationship, find a place of your own to live while you work through your feelings. Give yourself space and do not make the mistake of believing that you should not experience a sense of loss or grief simply because you made the choice to leave. You will have these feelings, and you have a right to experience them. Whether you grieve for your ex-partner or struggle with a sense of failure for the marriage in which you lived, you will need time to deal with your feelings and to come to terms with them. Committing yourself to a new partner without allowing yourself a breathing space will put tremendous emotional pressure on everyone involved and is likely to increase your own sense of guilt.

Surround yourself with those who love you and who accept that your decision was one you needed to make. Spend time discovering who you are as an individual. Do the things you enjoy doing, especially things that, perhaps, you could not do when you were married, such as reading a book in bed late at night, indulging in an aromatherapy massage or going out for a game of golf. Learning more about yourself and looking after yourself will increase your feelings of self-worth. Self-discovery will reinforce your sense of rightness in the decision you have made.

Value your freedom – you have earned it painfully. Begin to prepare the foundations for the new and fulfilling life that you so richly deserve.

4

Coping with Negative Emotions

I started stumbling around the house and dropping things. I would go up the stairs and I couldn't really feel them under my feet. I could no longer work in the evenings. I was too drunk. It took several years, but I began to realize that there was more to me than sinking into a bottle of wine. I knew I was better than this.

June, aged 52, separated

THE POWER OF love can inspire us to great heights of joy and achievement and of selflessness. When we love, we can be empowered to strive beyond our own limitations and to believe that we can attain the unattainable. But there is another side to this. When a partnership is destroyed, equally powerful emotions are released – negative emotions of a magnitude we had never before imagined possible. These feelings are initially intense, and they can be almost overpowering. They are the emotional debris resulting from the destruction of the entity that was the partnership, and, much like the fall-out of a nuclear explosion, the emotions take time to disperse.

Intense, negative emotions are difficult to handle. They are cumbersome, unwieldy and often impossible to deal with in a constructive manner. In the days following breakdown, it can seem as if our personal universe is beyond our control. Negative emotions naturally inspire negative coping strategies, and their intensity imposes profound pressure and discomfort, which beg for release. It seems as if our consciousness has been overfilled with a burden that is just too great for us to manage.

When such emotions are repressed, they often manifest themselves in physical illness, including headaches, gastric troubles or back pain. You may find it difficult to sleep, or you may find yourself eating too much for comfort or hardly eating at all. You may deaden the pain with alcohol or drugs. This can be a dark time, when black emotions threaten to engulf and overwhelm you. You may want to hide away and to isolate yourself in a cocoon, shunning contact with the outside world, while you attempt to deal with your emotions.

Releasing these emotions can be painfully difficult. Anger is often the most powerful and prominent emotion felt in the aftermath of breakdown, but acting out your anger is often socially unacceptable, particularly for women. Expressing anger isn't considered attractive, and revealing your anger is to behave with bad grace. Bottling up your anger, however, can mean that it eats away at you inside, seeping deep within to fester and present itself in other, less rewarding guises.

The forces of anger

Anger, rage and a desire for revenge – the process of relationship breakdown can yield a rich harvest of these emotions, which are the most potentially destructive forces in human nature, and the way in which we deal with them will have a crucial effect on the direction and quality of our future lives.

At times, however, anger can be a driving force. It can give us the strength to go on and the determination to fight and win our way past obstacles that seem insurmountable. When our world has fallen apart and there is little emotional nurture to give us sustenance, a diet of anger can keep us going. It can keep us, in the short term at least, from disintegrating and giving up altogether, without the will to begin again.

Feelings of anger and rage are a double-edged sword. In adversity, they can be a means of survival. Badly managed, though, they can cause destruction, lingering pain and permanent emotional scars to ourselves and our children. When we persistently translate our anger and our rage into a need for revenge, into verbal attack or physical aggression, we are setting up a vicious circle that allows the emotion to return to haunt us in a different form and to inflame the pain anew. We have all heard the term 'messy divorce', but what does the phrase really mean? It means that the anger is out of control, that one or both partners are using all the ammunition they have at their disposal to win a trophy of little inherent value: the last word, ownership of the battlefield, justice and vindication. When we win such trophies – and take pleasure in our success – we are providing ourselves with food on which future bitterness can thrive. It is important to learn to express anger, to push it out and then to let go of it so that we can get on with living.

Do these seem to be hard, 'easier said than done' words? Perhaps they are. Anyone who has experienced the breakdown of a relationship knows that anger can be both justified and healthy. With the pain of rejection or betrayal comes anger. In these circumstances anger is an instinctive reaction. We want to lash out at the person who has hurt us so badly, and we want to use whatever means are at our disposal to hit them and hit them hard. After all, fair's fair. Sensations of anger are normal during and after breakdown, and we cannot help experiencing them. They can, in fact, be of some benefit to us.

We are angry because the process of breakdown has made us into victims, and in becoming victims we have become powerless. Striking out at a partner isn't just about making them pay. It isn't just about getting even. It is about the exercise of power. If we can make a profound impact on the other person, we are no longer merely victims. We are powerful. We have snatched back some of the control we have lost, and we have proved that we can still draw an emotional response from the lost partner and are going to wring it out of them by whatever means we can. The psychology of anger is the psychology of power-play.

The exercise of power generates a sensation of strength, and the initial waves of anger can carry us above the bleakness of our grief. The anger helps us to hang on to one last shred of belief: that the marriage wasn't simply an illusion but was real once and that, in a negative sense, is real still. But feelings of anger must be tamed. The need to deal constructively with anger represents a critical point on the path to recovery. We need to master anger and manage it. Dealing with it is a watershed moment in our progress, and the way in which we deal with it matters in terms of our future well-being and in the future well-being of everyone involved. Until we come to terms with anger, digest it and let it pass away, we cannot move on in our own lives. As long as our anger is out of control, we are putting both ourselves and our children at risk of permanent emotional scarring.

When anger is out of control

A relationship does not usually break down overnight. In many cases, the two partners have already established a pattern of lashing out at each other, and the cycle will have built up long before the breakdown actually occurs. When a negative coping behaviour becomes established, the effects can be lasting. When it becomes part of the living entity that is the organism of partnership, it can turn back upon ourselves with damaging results. The method of coping with anger 'gels', and it generates worn grooves along which our anger flows. When we experience anger, the rage flows along those behavioural conduits that have been created for it through repetition. It follows the path of least resistance, the pathway that we have created through our own failure to understand and deal positively with our anger.

A harmful pattern of dealing with anger is difficult to change once it is established, but it is more harmful for us not to change it. We need to take an honest account of what anger can do when it is out of control, when we do not analyse where it is coming from or look for constructive ways in which to come to terms with it. Let us consider what it can do in the period leading up to the breakdown and afterwards in the months and years to follow. The effects of unmanaged anger are not attractive and they are not rewarding, but it is in our power to act now so that its effects do not continue to make their pernicious presence felt on our future. We will see that it is worthwhile to make the effort to control our anger.

June, a fifty-two-year-old research nurse, experienced the long-term effects of anger over the period of her twenty-three-year marriage. She married her ex-husband Matthew, who later became a consultant physician, in 1968, when she was twenty-three and he was twenty-five. Although they had three children within the first ten years of the marriage, June always worked because Matthew was not interested in being married to someone who was a traditional housewife and mother.

After the children were born, Matthew began to get 'hung up' about having sex while the children were around – at the time they were living in a small house – and about eight years after they were married, they virtually ceased having sexual relations, having instead what June describes as a 'brother and sister relationship'. In 1978 Matthew was posted to a consultancy and, after ten years of constantly moving house, they were able to settle down. For the first time, June was able to establish a close friendship with another woman. Then she discovered that Matthew and her friend were having an affair. 'It was shattering,' she recalls 'I was betrayed not only by him, but her as well. I was livid, furious, angry.'

June felt that the affair had happened because Matthew was dissatisfied with their lack of love-making, but they had never discussed this, and, in fact, the only time Matthew would discuss anything openly was when he was drinking. He said the affair had ended, but the pain and the anger were only just beginning. June, not much of a drinker, began to join in. 'Then, we both of us drank very heavily. Partly because I discovered that they didn't actually stop seeing each other for quite a long time, though he always denied it.... It just seemed easier to join in. It dulled the pain. But it was only many years later I realized it actually doesn't help and it made things far worse in every way.'

Drinking released emotions, and the pattern of drinking and arguing became established. When they drank, they argued. 'He is a very intelligent man and he had a tongue on him ... very sharp, very nasty. He would always tell me I was incapable of bringing up the children and I was an unsuitable mother. That I was thick and unintelligent. I began to believe it. And yet, I'd actually brought up the children on my own. He was never there. Ambition was his whole aim in life. But I suppose the reason why I was doing it myself was to prove that I was good. I was always trying to prove more and more. He wore me down into a little heap of ashes.'

An unexpected incident triggered a painful series of events in June's life. In 1990 she urgently required a hysterectomy, and while she was in the hospital, all the household routines collapsed. 'I could hear rows over the phone. They'd come to me crying. It was a nightmare.' She was feeling ill when she returned home and restored order. Six weeks later, she returned to work, although she was still far from well. But the drinking continued and the lashing out continued. 'Nothing was solved. Nothing. We went round in circles endlessly. The same old things were brought up night after night, and nothing ever happened. I became a total anorexic. I was receiving counselling by now. I just couldn't stop crying. I had a complete mental breakdown about a year later.'

June had been prescribed anti-depressants, but she held on to the prescribed medication for two weeks without taking the tablets. One evening she decided to take them all: 'It would get me better and it would finish me off and I would be out of all the misery.' But she admits that it was really a cry for help. June was admitted to hospital for psychiatric treatment. 'I remember it was a beautiful summer and I just listened to music very, very loudly. All I ever did was listen to music on my Walkman or car radio, so loud I must have woken up the whole city. In hospital, someone looked after me. They made me eat. They gave me routines, made me do occupational therapy. I was safe.'

Although she was still taking anti-depressants, she wasn't crying any more. For the first time, Matthew began to blame himself for what had happened to her. 'He was around all the time. All he ever did was lie about, crying. He'd just cry, all the time. I had gone beyond caring about him and what he felt or how he made me feel. I began to realize that for the children's sake, I had to survive.' Matthew had contributed to June's emotional destruction through his angry punishment, but June's collapse had, in turn, devastated Matthew. By that point, they were both empty, exhausted and deeply saddened. The children were shaken. It was over.

June and one of their daughters found Matthew a flat and furnished it for him. In 1991 he moved out of the family home.

Nevertheless, the aftermath of the anger played a significant role in the obstacles June faced in recovering from her breakdown. Slowly, one by one, she had to replace negative, set patterns of behaviour with new and more positive ones. She had to work to generate self-esteem. The destructive pattern had been maintained until no more damage could be done, and it had been buttressed by something else, the 'married for life' rule.

Why had June not ended the marriage when it became

characterized by anger and punishment, when the disease over-whelmed the organism? 'To me, marriage is absolutely for life, through thick and thin. One thing I never believed would happen to me is that I would be part of a broken marriage,' recalls June. But June and Matthew had effectively been 'breaking up' for years, continuing to act out their anger, through thick and thin, long after counselling might have helped them and long after separation should have been considered.

Never are we more at liberty, or better equipped, to destroy one another than in an intimate partnership. If we exercised integrity and self-discipline in dealing with our anger, we could do so much to prevent ourselves from inflicting lasting wounds and we could do so much to prevent the cloying type of guilt that can dog our heels for years into the future.

The urge to lash out

The period immediately following breakdown is when we are most susceptible to mismanaging our anger, and it is at this time that simple events can trigger an emotional explosion. This is because it is at this time above all that we realize that all our desperate attempts to preserve the marriage have failed and because at this time we have just cause to think of all the hurt our partner inflicted on us over the duration of the partnership. It is the time when even the gentlest of people is vulnerable to acting out their anger or rage through a desire for revenge. The partnership has crumbled around us and we stand surrounded by the rubble. Someone must be at fault, and someone, therefore, must pay.

We can toss our rationality and our better selves to the winds. It's easily done. When William's second wife, Jacqueline, left him, he was angry. He had been deserted for a second time and he felt betrayed. He felt that he had fulfilled his side of the partnership bargain by being a good husband, father and provider. And in return, he felt, she had treated him badly. She had had affairs during their marriage, and then she had left him. 'I felt totally betrayed. After all I had done for this girl,' he remembers. William, normally a kind and considerate person, a 'good guy', began venting his anger. He began to tell friends, anyone who would listen, what a terrible person Jacqueline was.

He remembers his behaviour at the time: 'I would bad-mouth her. That's all I did. I told them, "She did this and she did that." I'd be talking to people about what had happened and I was trying to blacken her character. And as much to make me look better. I sensed that they didn't know how to cope with the situation. They didn't know who to be loyal to. They didn't know what to say. They had no idea of what was happening to me. I didn't know myself at the time, so I can't blame them for that.'

There was an occasion, shortly after the breakdown, when William had to visit Jacqueline's parents to discuss the future of her son from before she and William had married. Her father knew nothing of his daughter's behaviour during the partnership and knew nothing of her affairs. Although William did not initially go with the intention of lashing out at Jacqueline, he found himself telling her parents simply in order to get his own back. 'Jacqueline's mum told her that she was very, very disappointed in her. Jacqueline broke down one night and phoned me and she said, "You told them. They know. They know." I will always remember those words. In some ways, I felt I'd redressed the balance.'

William attempted to 'redress the balance' in so many ways. He wanted publicly to prosecute Jacqueline for leaving him. He tried to kill the pain with another relationship. He retained custody of the children and had a separation agreement drawn up. In short, by taking aggressive, affirmative action, he was doing everything in his power to show he was in control. Getting an emotional reaction from Jacqueline gave him some satisfaction and a feeling of power. He felt that he wasn't the only victim. 'I wasn't in touch with my own feelings. All I wanted to do was get away from the pain,' he explained.

One evening William went to a dinner dance with the new girl he had become involved with. The following morning she made him coffee and served him breakfast. It is the sort of quiet, peaceful moment two people should enjoy together, but for William, it wasn't. 'She went up to the counter and I burst into tears. This wasn't like crying. This was sobbing. It was sobbing from the base of your boots. It just kept coming. I could hardly speak. We got in the car and ... I sat there and sobbed and sobbed for maybe two to three hours ... the girl with her arm around my shoulder. People had thought, "God, he's coping really well." But I didn't know what was growing inside. That morning was the breaking of the dam.'

Being angry and feeling betrayed are powerful forces, and they stretch our emotions to breaking point. Something has got to give. It is the hurt that engenders the desire for revenge, which is like a sickness feeding on our inner selves. We want to impose balance, justice and control, but we do it in ways that increase our own suffering. The greatest feat that any of us can achieve is to come to terms with our anger, to stop looking outwards towards the instrument of our pain, our ex-partner, and to look inside, where the real work needs to be done.

This is not to suggest that we should 'turn the other cheek' or that we haven't been victimized. Rather, it is to imply that the anger needs to be understood, and that the basic elements of that emotion need to be harnessed and processed. When the partnership is over, we are left with ourselves. The partnership that once existed is now an empty shell, and it is all too easy to fill that emptiness with flowing anger. But we must learn its limits, we must learn when it is no longer of use to us, and we must learn when to let go.

After his traumatic experience, William was telephoned by a friend who used to work with him. She asked how he was getting on, and he told her the truth. She suggested that he attend a support group for people who are separated, divorced or bereaved, and he remembers: 'It helped you to come to terms with the grief. Even to explain what it is about and why it is happening to you. It helped you to move along the road and make sure that you move through the process, learn to accept it, and move on with the rest of your life. It meant to free people to live again.'

And that's exactly what happened to William. He was freed to live again, after the betrayal and after the anger.

Dealing with anger constructively

Unless they have been through breakdown, no one can ever fully comprehend the depth and magnitude of emotion it can bring. If you have been there, you will know that the pain and hurt can drive you to do things that you would not normally even consider doing. It can drive your partner to do things that, normally, he or she wouldn't consider doing. It can leave you open-mouthed in amazement at what your partner has done. Never, in even your wildest dreams, did you suspect that this would happen to you.

But it has happened, and you are here. And that little bomb that is your anger is in your hands and is ticking away. It has to explode at some point. Whose lap are you going to drop it in? Or are you going to keep it? You are torn between letting it loose and bottling it up, or, worse, turning it against yourself in the form of self-hatred and self-punishing thoughts.

Learn to accept that your anger is an honest, healthy reaction to what has happened to you, but remember that it is what you do with it that matters. You can feel angry, but it is not necessary continually to punish yourself by putting yourself or anybody else down by taking offensive action. This kind of behaviour will undermine your integrity and hinder your progress in recovery. If fostered, it is the kind of behaviour that can lead to the persistent rot of bitterness. Give yourself permission to be angry, to feel it and to live it. Eventually you will no longer need it. You will let it pass. Recognize that this is a transient phase, a necessary stage in your reclamation of self, and that it is one aspect of a natural process of which you are part. Know that you will move on and that you will begin to rebuild.

Find ways in which to express your anger. This can be done in the form of writing – even keeping a diary will help. Drawing and painting are also positive forms of self-expression. Dancing is a means of physical expression and can be used to help you work through your anger. Select some music that you can listen to as loudly as you want, which will take you through your emotions and allow you to level out your feelings at the end.

Talking with a close friend or with a counsellor will give you opportunities to verbalize your angry fantasies about your ex-partner. You know you aren't going enact any of these fantasies, but talking about them will give you some release. If you are working through the anger by talking with a friend, agree before you begin that there will be a time limit for the discussion, then allow whatever feelings you have to rise to the surface openly and honestly and identify them for what they are. Give them a name.

Remember that as long as you are acting out revenge, as long as you are 'getting even' with your ex-partner, you are still hanging on to the relationship. 'Redressing the balance' can feel sweet, but there comes a time when you must focus inwards on what you really need. Although anger can protect us from the fear and vulnerability we feel when life seems beyond our control, it is also a form of restriction.

Looking for painkillers

When the intense pain of separation is first felt, a common reflex reaction is to look for something that will deaden it and make it go away. We look for the quickest and easiest method. The tide of emotions we feel – anger, self-hatred, worthlessness, shame and sadness – threatens to overwhelm us, and we need some form of anaesthetic to blot out these feelings and offer some respite.

William's painkiller took the form of finding a replacement for the wife who had left him. His motivation was not a desire to build a genuine relationship; he wanted a 'bandage' that would boost his self-esteem and take away the terrible feelings of worthlessness that assailed him. Ultimately, he had to recognize that this was a temporary and superficial solution and that he could not move forwards unless he turned around, looked inwards and faced the pain.

Jumping into a new relationship after losing a partner is a frequent reaction. Rushing out and finding a replacement means you are taking action and proving that you are all right. Filling the gaping inner wound with the salve of another person's affection and approval protects you, for a short time at least, from having to confront directly and with all your defences down the effects of the breakdown.

Drinking alcohol, taking drugs and eating too much are all ways of finding comfort and deadening pain, of escape and, often, of self-punishment and even of self-destruction. If you are a failure, if you are so worthless, you tell yourself, you deserve to be punished. Or this is how it may feel now. Whether or not your ex-partner knows what you are doing, these can also be a form of revenge by making him or her feel guilty: your behaviour is their fault. You are saying: 'Look what you have done to me. Look what you have reduced me to. You have destroyed me.'

How tempting it can be to wallow in these escapist fantasies. It is a sort of personal communion with our loss of partnership and, therefore, with our loss of self. There is an element of private self-indulgence about anaesthetizing ourselves against powerful emotions and our fear of the future. Over-indulging in drink, drugs or food can be done in private and alone. We have been wounded and need somewhere to hide, but unlike the hermit crab, we do not have our own protective shell to keep us safe from the outside world, so we look for some other solace.

Everyone – without exception – is susceptible to negative coping strategies following breakdown. After Tom left Caroline, she looked for comfort inside a bottle. 'I had never felt like such a huge failure in all my life. I drank quite a lot. It was to numb the pain. To make me sleep. I didn't go to the doctor. I would sit and polish off a bottle of wine. It was a crutch,' she remembers. June had already established a pattern of drinking behaviour while she was married to Matthew. It had started because Matthew drank and she felt she should join in. After the breakdown, the drinking continued. 'It was horrible. You wake up feeling ghastly. It was expensive. And it was pointless because nothing gets achieved while you are drinking.'

Some excessive behaviour at first is understandable. If we are realistic, we must accept that such behaviour is inevitable. However, the common theme is over-indulgence. The 'red alert', the warning signal, is when that behaviour, no matter what form it takes, is also prolonged. If your comfort eating or comfort drinking continues over a period of weeks and then months, you are establishing a pattern of harmful behaviour. Try to assess yourself. Is your weight dramatically increasing or decreasing? How often are you drinking and how much? Is it affecting your ability to work or to carry out daily routines? Do you feel compelled to over-eat or to have a drink? And, most importantly, do you feel out of control?

If the answer is 'yes', try not to panic. There is no behavioural pattern that cannot be altered, and there is no cycle that cannot be broken. Negative coping strategies are simply methods of dealing with emotional traumas or difficulties. They are symptoms, and, as such, they are not permanent. We simply need to replace them with positive coping strategies. If you feel you have established a pattern of negative behaviour, try counselling. Be honest with your counsellor about the extent and duration of the behaviour. If you are taking any form of medication, it should always be under the supervision of a doctor. Try to be a little accepting of yourself, for this behaviour is not a sign of weakness, and you would be both surprised and relieved if you knew how many other people were experiencing it, too.

Start developing some of your own positive coping strategies to take the place of the negative behaviour. Find one or two close friends who are willing to commit themselves for an agreed period of time to be available on the phone or in person to talk through your feelings, to offer you reassurance and to help you to feel better about yourself. Try some of the forms of self-expression mentioned previously, such as writing or dancing. Remember that alcohol consumption can increase depression. Instead of having a drink, try some light exercise. No one is asking you to stop drinking or to stop eating the foods you enjoy. The key is moderation.

'I want to be alone'

Wounded animals always run for cover. So do humans. We want to escape and hide ourselves away in order to punish or anaesthetize ourselves. We feel we have failed, and because the entity of our marriage has been destroyed, we no longer have an identity. We no longer know who we are. It is a confusing, frightening time. How should we behave? How should we conduct ourselves? We feel belittled and ashamed. When we no longer have control over our private universe, we can feel as uncertain and as powerless as children.

Where can we find safety and reassurance? One of the most common reactions to breakdown is self-imposed exile and isolation. Again, like the hermit crab, we look for a shell to protect our vulnerability, and there is no place like home. Being at home fulfils the most fundamental sense of security we have in our lives. Our homes represent safety and nurturing and offer protection.

Five years after the breakdown of her marriage, June still derives a sense of security from having her own space to be in. 'I think I'm always going to be a bit of a loner. I think there will still probably be some terrible moments but, on the whole, I prefer to be alone. I don't ever want to be hurt again.'

Although Caroline maintained contact with her friends, she, too, admits to having had a strong desire to hide away immediately after the breakdown: 'I wanted to be on my own. Cocooned. It was almost like a primitive instinct. To hide away. A primitive instinct to lick your wounds.'

The desire to 'cocoon' oneself after a traumatic experience is natural. There is a powerful need to heal, but there is also a sense of failure and shame that makes us shun going out into the world. When the intangible entity that was the partnership is torn down, we seek the security of something physical and tangible – four walls, bricks and mortar, and a roof: in short, a home.

There is, however, a risk in prolonging this form of isolation. At a time when we are subject to a vortex of confusing emotions and at a time when we need emotional nurture and support more than we have ever done, we can incline towards solitude. But in choosing solitude, we can become victims to the intensity of our emotional experiences. There is a danger that we will wallow in them, become steeped in them and allow them to overpower us.

The key to survival is balance. Understand that you need contact with others, who are going to offer you love and comfort. The tide of your emotions may vary, the emotions rising and falling in their intensity, but remember that you are grounded and that the beach on which the tide falls is always there, constant and permanent. Although you may feel vulnerable, allow yourself to be emotionally 'fed' by those who care for you. Choose who you allow into your world, but do not be afraid to take comfort when you need it, for you will, later on, be solid again.

When the time is right, the greatest gift we can give ourselves is freedom from the shackles of negative emotions – the freedom to move on.

5

Children

My son, David, is only just recovering from it. The breakdown was six years ago. He withdrew into himself then. For at least two or three years, you couldn't get a word out of him. I would tell people that he lived on the planet 'David'. That he was the only one who lived there. And that he only came home for his tea.

William, aged 50, separated

CHILDREN HAVE LITTLE or no control over their environment. To them, adults are the giants who rule and operate the universe in which they live, who structure their lives, create a sense of security and provide physical and emotional nurture. During the breakdown of a marriage, children can become silent victims, even with the most well-meaning of parents. When we are involved in splitting up with our partner, we are totally absorbed in the process, devoting all our efforts to managing our own mental and emotional state, and to surviving.

While we are attempting to pick up the pieces of our own lives, we have little to offer our children and may even feel it is impossible to meet their needs. The time they need us most is when we are at our lowest ebb, when we are crippled by our own need for support and nurturing. We are human, we are not gods, but our children perceive us as having god-like powers over their destinies. As difficult and painful as the after-effects of breakdown can be, we need to set an example for them to emulate and to maintain as much of a sense of security for them as we can throughout the transition.

How children perceive us managing the breakdown is vital to their future. They are small observers to an adult trauma, but this does not mean they do not feel, see or experience intense emotional reactions. As adults, we have layers of experience and have learned coping skills. If you are now feeling that it is almost impossible to deal with the overwhelming trauma of breakdown, try to imagine what your children are experiencing. Their world is being torn apart, but they have no power to end the suffering.

It is tempting to turn your mind from these thoughts because of the guilt that they may inspire. Knowing that your children are suffering through a trauma that has been created by you and your partner can make you feel deeply uncomfortable, and the knowledge can cause a secondary explosion of guilt and failure. You already have so much to deal with that you are as vulnerable as your own children, as powerless to turn the tide of events and as confused as they are. How can you help them if you are managing to hang on to your own sense of self by your remnants of will-power?

First, you must accept the truth. Never underestimate the impact that your breakdown will have on the children. If you accept this as a reality, you can genuinely help them to adjust. It is in your power to prevent long-term emotional scars by acting positively now. You can take real comfort in this: if your children observe you adjusting and coping well, they will emulate your behaviour. Strong, reassuring relationships between children and splitting parents prevent the trauma from re-emerging in their later years. You must act to prevent wounds from becoming scars.

Even if it requires an act of will to turn your attention to the children and help them deal with what is happening to them, it is important that you make every effort to do so.

When children become casualties

When we break up, we involve the children in our anger in different ways, but we should work to avoid this at all costs. If young children are in the position of witnessing their parents at war, it will seem like the clash of the Titans. Everything will be larger than life to them, and the conflict between their parents will be a terrifying experience. Their whole world will seem to be falling to pieces around them. The breakdown of their parents' relationship will make an impression on their consciousness that will remain for years to come if not for their entire lives.

It is understandable that there will be arguments, disagreements and displays of anger during the breakdown and afterwards. Even the occasional loss of control over anger is understandable, but we must never forget how much children absorb and how our expressions of rage can be powerfully disturbing for them.

Although June emphasizes that they argued in front of the children only occasionally, the cycle was having an effect. 'It was mainly at night. Though they must have been aware of it because they used to go to their bedrooms early and just stay there. I think we had no time for them for a while. It was as though they weren't there.' Only when she returned from the hospital did June realize the terrible effect that she and Matthew had had on the children. She had to reassure them.

It was only after her recovery from her own mental breakdown that June was fully able to comprehend the effects of their behaviour on the children. 'Gradually I got better and came back home. I had shaken the children dreadfully. And it was only then that I saw what we had done, what the two of us had done. My daughter had sadly failed her A-levels and my other daughter had become quite a mental wreck about us both. We never got it back together again after that.' The wounds took a long time to heal. Today, the children are well-adjusted but, from time to time, June sees evidence of the permanent effects of parental warfare and of Matthew's critical, angry behaviour.

There is another, all too common method of involving our children in disputes with our ex-partner. It is most frequently seen in the months and years following breakdown, and it involves manipulating young children. We use young children to give us power over our ex-partner and as a means to gain inches of valuable ground on the battlefield. If the children are older, we may attempt to use them as allies, feeding them with selective information, offering all the reasons they should reject our ex-partner and using them as psychological weapons with which we can inflict pain and maintain some power and control over the life of our ex-partner.

When Sara left her marriage in 1977, she also left their six-year-old adopted daughter, Kirsty, in the marital home with husband George. 'I had left my husband and I hadn't taken my child. A number of people said, "Oh, I could never do that. I could never leave my child." But I left her behind because I couldn't provide for her. I had thirty-five pounds in my pocket and I was living in a room.' Sara also wanted to maintain consistency in Kirsty's life. She wanted her to sleep in the same bed and attend the same nursery school. Her intentions were commendable, but she was now vulnerable to unexpected punishment. George was angry: his wife had deserted him, she had been unfaithful, and his wounds were fresh and urging him to act.

Their separation agreement had allowed Sara to have Kirsty every alternate weekend, and Sara would spend one half-day a week working in Kirsty's nursery to be near her. Late in the week, when it was Sara's 'off' weekend, George would often ring and say he wanted Sara to take Kirsty anyway. If Sara had already made plans and declined the offer, George would tell Kirsty, 'Mummy doesn't want you.' This would reinforce Kirsty's insecurity: Mummy had left the marital home, and Mummy didn't want her.

Children do not take into account separation agreements or visitation schedules when it comes to wondering if they are loved. They have no defences in their parents' attempts to use them as pawns in the game of angry manipulation. They are simply bewildered and wounded by the crossfire.

Sara remembers: 'Kirsty was misled. Her image of me was corrupted. Then, at the same time, I'd fight back against him through her. I'd ask her, "What did Daddy say?" And then I would tell her, "No, that's not right. This is the truth." I'd explain to her what he'd done to me, that he had made me leave. I'd complain to her that he was manipulating me and warn her to watch out. It was wrong. It left a permanent mark on her. We should have been mature enough to keep her out of it.'

Kirsty is now twenty-three, and she and her mother are very close. But Sara has seen that Kirsty suffers from a strong sense of insecurity, particularly in her own relationships, and she feels that she and George had a lot to do with this and that this is the sad fruit of the seeds sown by the parents in their battle to gain points after the breakdown of their marriage. The seeds bore other fruit, too. Years later, the manipulative behaviour of the parents, using the child as a conduit of their angry feelings towards each other, returned in the form of guilt, the guilt that Sara feels for her, now adult, child. The guilt that will never go away.

It is important that we look for ways in which to channel our anger that do not involve children. Using children in this way creates only pain, confusion and insecurity for them, and it teaches them that to love both parents is to know the meaning of guilt, for to love one parent implies disloyalty to the other.

Because our children bind us to our ex-partner, in one way or another, for life, we can go on punishing our ex-partner indefinitely and thereby depriving our children of their right to a fulfilling relationship with both parents. This may bring some short-term satisfaction to us, but it also means that the parents' actions may rebound on the children because we have opened the door to the perpetuation of a negative cycle, of a set pattern of behaviour, which they can lock into as they grow to adulthood and begin their own relationships.

Mediation over children can do much to reduce acrimony. If you are concerned about your future security, remember that there are great differences between acrimony and firmness, between retribution and fairness. Negotiation entails the sensible, wise and farsighted application of the tools – not weapons – that we have at our disposal. Anger and revenge have no place at the negotiating table and no place in the crucial decisions that will affect our lives and the lives of our children in the years to come.

Above all, if you have children, protect them while the breakdown of your relationship is happening.

Protecting your children from anger

No matter how angry he felt, William had the foresight not to involve the children in his acting-out behaviour, even though he was the resident parent, which gave him considerable influence over their perceptions. When his daughter Rachel was just ten years old, they had an open discussion on the subject. He said to her: 'I don't quite know why your Mum and I broke up, but I am beginning to learn. But one thing I can tell you is that your Mum loves you. She does not like conflict. When it came to the breakdown, rather than face conflict, because it is so terrible to her, she did what she did. She didn't leave you because she didn't love you. She left you because she couldn't fight for you.'

He then showed her a line he had read about personality characteristics, which he thought described Jacqueline well. 'It said that, without being aware of it, this type of person can sacrifice their spouse, their children and even themselves for the sake of peace,' recalled William. Rachel read it and then responded: 'That means my Mum still loves us, Dad. She didn't go because she doesn't love us.' And later, she was to say, 'When I'm at Mum's, that is my home. When I am here with you, this is my home.'

'It was then I put the white flag up. Out of the mouths of babes,' said William warmly.

If you have already had angry or rage-filled disputes around the children, make an agreement with your ex-partner to put an end to such wrangling. Refuse, from this time onwards, to become involved in arguments when the children are present. Implement damage control by encouraging them to talk about what is happening and how they feel about it. Reassure them and soothe them. If you think they need counselling, offer it to them. If they see you and your ex-partner coping constructively with the transition, they will accept it and adjust to it positively.

Emotional dependence on children

During and after a breakdown, we are also more likely to depend on our children for support as if they were adults, attempting to cement their loyalty and draw on their strength. When our partner is gone, our source of support and comfort goes too. The safe and secure entity of the partnership has been destroyed, and we are left frightened and insecure. When this happens, it seems natural to turn to other sources of comfort, sources who are always there – the children.

Vicky, who is now fifty-nine, was married for thirty-one years. In 1988 she learned that her husband, Bill, was seeing another woman. When she first found out about the affair, Vicky felt as if her universe had collapsed. 'I was shocked,' she said. 'I felt as if the world had crumbled away beneath my feet. I wanted to rush about. I wanted to find out more about the affair. I know I went for a walk and I couldn't take in the surroundings as I passed them by. I did notice it was a lovely, hot day and I thought, "How can it be this beautiful when my world has fallen to pieces?"'

Bill decided to leave, but Vicky couldn't bear to let go. After investing so many years in the marriage, she hoped that she could find a way to salvage it, and she therefore allowed Bill – who could not make up his mind to end the marriage – to spend some weekends with her. When they were together, they lived as husband and wife. Then Bill would return to his other partner. Yet Vicky hung on to that shred of hope for four years, hoping that he would come back. It was only when Bill pressured her to sign over to him her interests in the marital home that Vicky realized he would never return and that she would no longer have a home. In 1992 she went to see a lawyer and brought proceedings for divorce.

Vicky and Bill had six children. The two youngest were still living at home when Bill had first moved out. Tim was nine and the elder, Greg, was a teenager. The four years before Vicky brought divorce proceedings were a crucial period of adjustment for her and the children. After Bill was gone, Vicky found herself turning to Greg for comfort. 'My son helped me a lot. I think I needed a lot of reassurance from him. I don't think I could have behaved any differently at the time. But I was still running the house as I had always been. I used to say, "Do you think he'll come back, Greg?" And he used to say, "Yes, I think so." I would be happy then. He suddenly became responsible for the house in a way.'

Vicky felt she could not help herself. She drew the children close. In a world of uncertainty, where she had lost the very thing that gave herself a sense of personal value – the marriage – she turned to what remained – her son. How could Greg possibly know if his father would return? But he said the words because they reassured his mother, and the reassurance made her feel better and stronger. But how was he feeling? Did he not need reassurance too? Did he not have questions? Did he not feel uncertainty?

When a relationship breaks down, we feel pain and loss – after all, it was our partnership. In most cases, children are not the cause of the partnership, but the result of it. They are the living expression of the union. We feel that the breakdown is primarily happening to us, not to our children, and the experience makes us focus inwards. We are just trying to survive, which can take all our mental and physical resources, and it is devastating to entertain the idea that our offspring may be suffering as much as we are. But if we do not get to grips with this possibility, it is probable that we will blindly turn to them in our time of need, afraid to let go of them and afraid to allow them to be close to our ex-partner because we could not bear to lose the children, who are our only remaining source of love and security.

Using our children as sources of reassurance places a terrible burden on them. This is especially so if the children are very young. We absorb their energy at a time when they need it most, and we impose on them, yet again, divided loyalties. We do not realize that they may be desperately trying to make sense of their own feelings of loss, abandonment and rejection. When we depend on our children for reassurance, we are drawing from an emotional reservoir that has not evolved to its full potential, and because it has not fully evolved, it is more vulnerable to permanent disfigurement. In addition, because they are developing, children perceive emotional events more intensely, which is why childhood memories have a special, powerful quality. Childhood is the time when the emotional anatomy of a potential adult is at its most tender and most vulnerable to emotional experiences.

Everything that happens before and during a breakdown is experienced by children directly, without the filter of reasoning abilities that an adult is able to bring to bear. Because children do not have a wider framework of understanding on which to call, they are confused and bewildered by what is happening around them. Tempting though it may be, it is vital that we do not turn to our children for emotional support. What is vital is that we understand what they are experiencing and how they are experiencing it.

Children's reactions to breakdown

Although children know what they are feeling, they often find it difficult to express themselves, and this leaves them with the problem of how to deal with their emotions. Research by the William Gladden Foundation in the United States, published in 1989 in *The Effects of Divorce on Children*, has revealed some of the problems faced by children whose parents separate.

Children's reactions to breakdown will, of course, depend on their age as well as on their individual character. The entire universe of children up to about the age of six is focused on their parents, and the breakdown of their parents' relationship can leave them feeling confused and frightened of being abandoned. They may cry a great deal and cling to one or both parents, and they may even blame themselves for the split. When the children are between seven and twelve years old, there may be tantrums, and they may feel a powerful sense of loss and rejection. They may also feel torn between their two parents. Adolescence is a difficult enough period of adjustment for most children. When they are in their early teens, they are trying to adjust to dramatic physical, emotional and social transformations. They are vulnerable to feelings of insecurity and rejection. They may have dramatic mood swings or withdraw from those who are close to them. Peer pressure can mean that they are ashamed of their parents' divorce, and they may feel angry and resentful. Older teenagers may be better able to cope and understand, but their parents' separation may lead them to doubt their own capacity to have well-adjusted relationships.

If children are not helped to make a positive adjustment to breakdown, parents may be forced to deal with the consequences for years to come. It is a terrible experience for children to feel that they must deal with their own emotions alone. If we do not recognize their needs and help their efforts to work through what is happening to their world, they may be haunted for the rest of their lives by unresolved questions. It is vital that you include your children in the recovery process, by helping them to understand what is happening around them and by encouraging them to express their own fears and anxieties.

Every child is going to feel the effects of the breakdown in a different way, but no child is too young or too old not to be affected by it. We need to be observant, and we need to recognize how and when help is needed.

When his first marriage had broken down in 1967 William had allowed his children to stay with their mother. While they were growing up, he found it difficult to deal with being the absent parent and with visitation arrangements. When his second marriage to Jacqueline ended in 1989, therefore, he knew what problems the absent parent faced. 'I had been through it before – being an absent parent,' he said. 'I didn't want to have to pick the kids up on a Saturday again and wander around town centres and skating rinks. I couldn't do that again. It was terrible. It was like wandering around like a lost soul, trying to keep two children amused.'

When William and Jacqueline broke up, their two children, Rachel and David, were seven and eight years old. This time, his wife agreed to William becoming the resident parent, and the children remained with him. Rachel adjusted to the breakdown well. She was able to talk through her feelings with her father and to ask questions about what was happening. William answered them as carefully and honestly as he could. 'I told her that her Mum would always be there at weekends and that she could always go and visit her. She's an amazing girl. She learned to come to terms with it.'

David did not find it so easy, however. He withdrew to what William calls 'the planet David', and he began to have problems at school. 'The school telephoned and said they were worried about my son. They thought he was depressed. He wouldn't talk. And, even though he's a bright lad, I have had school difficulties with him ever since. He's fifteen now and it's only recently that he's begun to talk with me. We're beginning to hit it off.'

As parents, we love our children and we want what is best for them, and the guilt that we feel if they are harmed because of the breakdown can gnaw away at us for years. But this is not the way it has to be. Relief and confidence can be found in the knowledge that children can adjust well and learn to accept the breakdown as an obstacle that the family can transcend together. A child's fear of abandonment and feelings of loss, anger, confusion and rejection can be transformed into understanding. Learning from this experience can provide them with knowledge to deal with the real world, to adjust and to move forward.

Helping your children to adjust

When you break up, children experience an almost overwhelming feeling of bewilderment. Never underestimate how much they are taking in about what is happening around them and about what is happening between you and your partner. What and how much they perceive will play an important part in their ability to adjust to the dramatic changes that they are experiencing. But they must be helped to digest and synthesize those experiences and to cope with the wounds so that they do not turn into scars that will mark them for life.

How you deal with your own feelings will affect your children. If they see you reaching out for help and support, you are setting an example for them – a good example. Make yourself available to them if – and when – they want to ask questions. Many separating parents are so caught up with what is happening to themselves that they withdraw from their children. Like June and Matthew, they don't have time for them. Caroline felt that even though she had 'two lovely kids', she had lost everything.

Children can be more traumatized by breakdown than adults because they have yet to learn the psychological mechanics of adjusting to dramatic changes in significant relationships. They do not know that the breakdown of their parents' relationship is not the end of the world and that their recovery is not only possible but inevitable. However, if you do not respond to them when they want to talk and when they need help in piecing together what is happening to them, they may withdraw and stop talking altogether. Remember that what children need above all is consistency and familiarity. They need reassurance, and they need someone to be available just for them. So, in addition to making yourself available for the children, it is helpful if you can also appoint another family member or someone who is close to the family who will be supportive and on whom the children know they can rely and to whom they can talk. It is also advantageous if this person is independent and won't take sides with you or with your partner in any discussions. This will encourage your children to ask questions without feeling frightened or threatened by what they are feeling and experiencing.

Never forget that children are a living bond that will exist between you and your partner for life. Give yourself the satisfaction of being able to look back on your handling of this stage of your life without guilt. Even if you are still acting out your angry feelings towards your ex-partner, make an agreement with him or her that, as parents, you will not involve the children in painful interactions. Agree to cooperate whenever the children are concerned. Remember that very young children may blame themselves for the breakdown. Make sure that they understand that the breakdown of the relationship is not their fault, and make sure that both you and your partner explain this to the children.

If you and your partner demonstrate cooperation in front of the children, it will help them to come to terms with the transition and help them to accept that what has happened is part of a process of development rather than the end of the world.

Teach your children that even though everything around them appears to be in a state of flux, there is a consistent central point in their lives. Although one parent will be moving away and other things may change, the emotional bond each child has with both parents remains unchanged. Explain to them that it is the quality, not the quantity, of time spent with them that matters. When the non-resident parent is visiting, it is vital that their emotional closeness with the children is maintained, and both parents need to encourage their children to sustain positive, loving relationships. Such relationships will help to stem the flow of feelings of loss, and it is this sense of loss or abandonment that can damage children in the long term.

The breakdown of their parents' relationship generates a range of emotions in children, from bewilderment to fear and insecurity. If their parents' world is destroyed, then so is theirs. And children's perception of time is different from that of adults. For children it can seem as if this period of uncertainty and unhappiness will last for ever. Your emotional closeness can be reassuring, but your emotional dependence can steal from them their own freedom to deal with what has happened. Be there for them; listen to them. If you feel that you are not, if only temporarily, capable of listening, find someone who can listen. Well-grounded, open relationships are vital for a strong sense of self-worth.

These suggestions may seem easier said than acted upon. How can you possibly reassure your children when you cannot even reassure yourself? How can you offer attention and understanding when you are so much in need and when you are struggling with the confusion, fear and insecurity brought by the loss of your own partnership? What you are feeling is understandable, and your needs deserve to be met. You need comfort and space to work through your own grief, and you need to take the time and make the effort to ensure that you get them. Being kind to yourself is essential if you are to survive the storm.

But keep this in mind: you are the fundamental power in your children's universe. However, this power brings responsibility. Even if it takes a great deal of strength, it is worth helping your children survive this change in their lives. Remember to control the intense negative feelings you have towards your ex-partner so that you can help them realize that their world is not going to fall apart, that they are loved and that they have every reason to feel secure because you are there for them.

6

Dealing with Other People

*They were just so shocked. Because our friends had this
image that we were very happy – which we had been,
I would say, for most of the time. And then, of course,
as soon as I started telling them, I would break down. It
was all so raw then. It was like breaking the news of a
death to somebody. It was just like that.*

Caroline, aged 41, separated

WE ARE NEVER fully prepared for how others will react to the
news of the breakdown of our marriage and how they will
deal with us in the days, weeks and months to come. It is not
uncommon to feel a sense of shame and embarrassment when we
break the news, for there is always the shadow of 'failure' looming
over us.

Like children, we have an overwhelming need for reassurance,
understanding and love, but when we tell our family and friends
about the breakdown, we sometimes feel as if we have let them
down. We may even find ourselves comforting *them* as if it were
their loss. This is because family and friends also have expectations
of our partnership. Their perception of us as individuals is based
on the knowledge that we are married or part of a couple. It is
almost as if they draw from the stability of our partnership a
secondary sense of their own security. How they interact with us is
based on an awareness, consciously expressed or not, of our
'coupledom'. It is probable that if we are in a partnership, most of
our friends will also be couples. Because they identify with us and
we with them, our breakdown will have an effect on each and every
relationship and reflect back a complex and distorted image of
confusion and discomfort.

If the partnership can be regarded as the structure in which we
have lived, our relationships with others could be seen as making

up the landscape surrounding it – that is, its context. Taking the metaphor further, the landscape is an essential part of the structure and contributes to the overall entity. Imagine your partnership and the partnerships of your friends and colleagues as a group of buildings, set in the beauty and continuity of a village surrounded by green countryside. If one of the structures within that village is derelict, it is not only the inhabitants of the devastated structure who will be affected. The other inhabitants of the community will see and feel the blight on their own horizons and on their once-continuous landscape. They will see it as they peer out from the security of their own partnerships. And perhaps they will feel frightened.

Your breakdown will leave them with three choices: to attempt to rebuild your partnership; to accept and adapt to the change; or to remove the problem so that their image of their lifestyle remains unimpaired and unthreatened.

Little do we realize that the nature and quality of our friendships are, to a large extent, defined by our status, single or partnered. This is not to say that our friendships do not have an essential quality that is based on a bond between us as individuals, and it is not to suggest that our parents, brothers and sisters and other relations will love us any less because we have become single again. What it means is that they may also experience loss. They will have to come to terms with the separation. If we have developed a 'coupled identity' and if the partnership provided structure and meaning to our lives, the people close to us will have played a role in that identity, structure and meaning, and our partnership will have played a part in their lives. Breakdown will bring this interrelationship into the open.

You should be prepared for the fact that breakdown will bring significant changes in your relationships with those who are close to you, and that it will bring about a comprehensive transformation in the social context within which you live. You should expect the unexpected. Parents, in-laws and friends may put pressure on you and your ex-partner to mend the relationship – on the other hand, they may not. They may be shocked, stunned, baffled or tearful. Some friends may feel threatened: they may feel that if your marriage has broken up, theirs is at risk, too. In-laws with whom you have nurtured close and abiding relationships over the years may simply disappear from your life. Friends with whom you have shared so many dinner parties, outings, warmth and laughter may simply fade away over the coming months. If the break with your partner is acrimonious, friends will be confused in their loyalties and the event will be confusing and uncomfortable for everyone involved.

Facing first reactions

Just when we need support, affection and empathy the most, we find that we have to deal with the reactions of others. At first, they may share in our shock and grief. Then things begin to change – some changes are subtle, others less so. This is another dimension of the disintegration of the partnership and one with which we must learn to cope. Our relationships with significant others are like familiar objects. When our relationship breaks down, we reach out, as it were, into the surrounding landscape for the comfort of familiarity. We are frightened and alone, and we fumble in the dark, seeking the comfort of familiar shapes and forms to reassure us. Yet we find that they are changing just as we reach out to them. Often, where we expected to find love and support, we find only an emptiness. But, where we presumed there was emptiness, we may find an unexpected source of warmth and sustenance.

When our relationship breaks down, the landscape of our relationships with others will shift, sometimes beyond recognition and sometimes in ways that we cannot control. It is important to be as prepared for this change as possible. We must be observant and make an effort to understand that the negative reactions we may encounter are not evidence of our own failure but manifestations of other people's inability to cope with the breakdown – that is, to cope with what our breakdown means to them.

When Caroline had finally accepted that her marriage was over, one of her first actions was to contact friends. She knew that this was going to be difficult, for everyone thought they were the 'perfect couple'. Their first reactions were shock and denial. Caroline likened it to imparting news of a death. But she needed their support because both her parents were dead and she an only child. Her friends were her family. 'They were just totally stunned. But I had to tell everybody. I needed support ... and to talk. All I wanted to do was to analyse what had happened. Everybody thought he'd had a mid-life crisis because it was sort of fashionable to think that and he was at that age. And I wanted the comfort. I had no family. I still do feel that very keenly. No brothers or sisters to turn to.'

Caroline's friends were supportive over the coming weeks. For the first six months, she was still hoping her husband would return, and one friend and his girlfriend even acted as go-betweens, attempting to persuade Tom to mend the break. No one wanted to accept that the marriage was over.

When Hugh's wife Annie left him, he thought about a way to tell his parents. He was meeting his father one evening and he simply said: 'By the way, Dad, Annie's moving out today.' His father passed on the news to Hugh's mother, but in-depth discussion of a major, traumatic event in Hugh's life was avoided and the subject was deftly side-stepped. His parents were embarrassed, disappointed and let down, and the end of Hugh's marriage was dealt with as if it were an unsavoury incident. No one had the opportunity to share their feelings, their concerns or their fears, and there was no opportunity through which mutual comfort might be offered. Hugh was worried for his parents. 'I didn't feel I could burden my parents with it. So I bottled it up inside and kept up a front.'

Parents' reactions can vary. Although many will respectfully stay out of it, voice their concern or simply offer their support, others will bring pressure to bear for a reconciliation. We may even find ourselves feeling responsible for their distress, and they could make us feel guilty or ashamed about the breakdown, fuelling our sense of failure. This can be difficult, for, as we saw with Caroline's marriage, parents and in-laws can be part of the cement that keeps the relationship together even in troubled times. It wasn't until both Caroline's parents and Tom's mother were dead that Tom broke away. This was more than coincidental. When she found out about Tom's first affair, Caroline could not bear to confide in her friends or her parents. 'My parents loved him. How on earth could I tell my parents this had happened? I couldn't bear to see their faces.'

When their mutual friends learned of the breakdown, Hugh was shocked by the response, or rather, the lack of it. 'At the wedding there were a hundred people. I never heard a word from any of them. Not one person rang up to say, "How are you?"' When his wife left him, the friends disappeared just as if they had never existed. There were other disappointments, too. It left him feeling isolated and alone with the burden of grief. He said: 'I felt that my life was water in a glass. The glass had been pushed over and the water had gone everywhere. No matter how hard I tried to push the water back in the glass, I could not get it back in there.' And, as he was to discover, it was not a task he could achieve alone.

Dealing with rejection and prejudice

Emma, now a forty-seven-year-old registered nurse, met and married her husband David in South Africa in 1974. She had gone to that country with two friends on a year's contract after they had completed their midwifery training. While she was dating David, both her friends announced that they were getting married and Emma felt that this, to some extent, influenced her decision to get married too.

Within six months, Emma was pregnant with her only child, but after the birth of their son their sex life became strangely 'non-existent'. It was several years before Emma was to discover that David was a homosexual. There were other problems, too.

'He needed to have total control. Control of my life, completely,' she remembered. Emma was not allowed to have her own bank account. Her wages from nursing were given over to David, and if she wanted money, she had to ask for it. If she asked for it, he would tell her she didn't need it. She was not allowed to drive. Years passed by, and slowly she was worn down until she felt weak, insignificant and useless. She was trapped. 'It takes a long, long time to realize it and by then you are so demoralized. I remember, one night, they had evacuated a ward and they were painting it. I remember going in there, in the dark, and sitting on the paint tins and crying my eyes out.' When she finally confronted him about his homosexuality, he admitted it but exploited her feelings of inadequacy. 'He said that it was because of the way I had treated him that he had turned to men. I just had to put up with it really. I should have gone, but I had no money to go. He also said he wouldn't let me take my son out of the country. I felt, again, if I behaved myself and was good, he might change.'

The marriage lasted eighteen years. For Emma, the pressure had been building to an intolerable level. During the last two years of the marriage, between 1990 and 1992, she had taken comfort in over-eating. She was 5 foot 3 inches tall, but by the summer of 1992 she weighed 16 stone. David's secret was destroying what was left of her. Emma decided it was time for change and at last reached out for help. She went through the telephone book and organized an appointment with a hypnotherapist to attempt to lose unwanted weight. The decision was to change her life for ever.

'I hadn't consciously gone with the idea that I was going to talk. I just wanted help with dieting. She was great. She really was. It felt like a betrayal [of David] initially. But it was a big release.' Emma lost 5 stone in three months, and in August 1992, she told David she'd had enough and asked him to leave.

After he was gone, she began to telephone their friends and break the news – about David's homosexuality and the breakdown. 'Some of them said they knew. Some of them were quite surprised. Some of them I have never heard from since.' In talking to their friends, she found herself almost wishing David had physically abused her, so that they could understand the pain. 'It sounds funny, but then people would know how I felt,' she said. 'If they saw bruises, they would know I was bruised.'

Emma also found that existing friendships can easily fade away as soon as the news is given out. Because she had ended her marriage, it was expected that she should simply get on with her life. 'I don't think that they think of it as a grieving process. They think of it more as something you chose to do. And, you should be happy about it. I think they were afraid of facing up to things, of facing up to the issues. They just didn't want to know. It made me angry, really. They really don't have any perception at all.'

Then come the experiences of prejudice and of misconception and the slights that dig into our already wounded self-esteem. Reactions from our friends can be evidence of their own fears, yet they strike us when we are at our most vulnerable. Four months after David had gone, a friend's husband offered to help Emma with some work around the house. 'He was doing some DIY for me and was due to come around about nine thirty in the morning. About eight thirty, his wife rang and said, "Bill is coming around. He'll be there in an hour. Make sure you are dressed."' Emma was hurt and shocked. 'The ones that have felt threatened, I do not see any more. I thought, "If that's the way she feels, she's not going to change and I just don't need it."'

It is not unusual for women in particular to be viewed as a threat by some married women friends. After all, aren't all separated or divorced women desperately seeking a replacement for the husband they have lost? Aren't they looking for a man, any man? Wouldn't it be wise to put our husbands safely under lock and key whenever our separated or divorced girlfriend comes to visit?

Stealing husbands is rare. Just out of one broken relationship, women are raw and in need of support. They are less likely to want to jump into a new relationship than to look for support and understanding. They want time to heal, but ignorance of the true magnitude of the trauma of breakdown leads to many hurtful misconceptions, including the 'divorced-women-are-easy' myth. It's a sad truth that, if some wives fear losing their husbands to the woman 'refugees' of a breakdown, some husbands believe that they can capitalize on their new-found single status and vulnerability, apparently regarding separated women as willing and easy prey.

When June's twenty-three-year marriage to Matthew ended, she turned to one couple for support, but she was soon to drop the friendship completely. 'He [the husband] was one of three married men who homed in immediately, asking, "was I free for a bit on the side?" after Matthew had moved out. I was so appalled, annoyed and disgusted with the whole of mankind. I just could not cope with that. I kept a big distance from the couple after that. I realized that's why divorced women have a bad reputation ... that they're after all the men available. It's the married men who are after them.'

The whole process of our breakdown can cause some people to shy away, while others look to gain from our loss. And these people can leave us feeling insulted or rejected, angry and hurt all over again. Rejection can intensify our feelings of worthlessness, and we begin to think: 'Well, even my friends don't want me.' We are bewildered, wondering whether our friends had ever valued us in the first place. After all, we invested so many years in our friendships, what was the point of it? Can we just be suddenly dumped or even gradually weaned away as simply as that?

Any woman who has suddenly become single again is also at risk of becoming a social pariah for no other reason than the fact that she is on her own, but it should not be presumed that men do not also experience prejudice or rejection. They simply manifest themselves in different ways. When Hugh attempted to discuss his breakdown with colleagues at work – the same colleagues with whom he lunched and spent time – he felt as if a wall had gone up. 'I felt there was an attitude towards me that they didn't want to confront the problem. That if you do not confront the problem of people breaking up or divorcing, it won't happen to you. We'll talk about the weather rather than address the situation and hopefully, it will go away. To be honest, until now, that would probably have been my attitude if the roles had been reversed between me and people at work.'

The pattern of our relationships begins to shift, often dramatically, around us. The after-shock of the impact of the breakdown can send shock-waves throughout our entire social world, and we can only stand helpless as familiar objects – our friendships – alter beyond recognition.

But it is vital to remember that what we are witnessing does not reflect on our own character or on our own worth. Although there may be, to some degree, an element of 'scales falling from our eyes' as we see how others react to our separation, it is important that other people assume responsibility for their own feelings. At this time, we have to look to our own needs, and we must sift through the rubble of our relationships and find what is good for us and discard what is not.

Letting go of those you don't need

Just as we have expectations of our partnership, we also have expectations of other, important relationships. We must be prepared for potential distress, embarrassment or discomfort from our friends and relatives, and we must be able to distinguish between those on whom we can depend and those who cannot deal with the crisis. How friends comprehend and deal with the breakdown will be, to some degree, dictated by their own experiences. If they have not been through a breakdown themselves, their understanding may lack a valuable dimension and an empathy that might otherwise exist.

We must learn to be open to unexpected sources of support and to deal with the reality that many existing relationships will not survive the transition.

Kate, a forty-six-year-old social worker, was married for twenty-three years. Over the years there had been, on and off, periods when her husband, Ray, would physically abuse her. He made her believe that it was her fault and that she had made him angry, and Kate kept hoping that the abuse would stop. Finally, one night in 1992, Kate made the decision to end it. 'He'd had an awful lot to drink and had brought home a take-away curry. I was very annoyed and said that if he was going to stay out all night, he should have told me so. He threw the curry at me and hit me again. That was it. Something finally snapped. He stormed out and I threw all of his clothes into black bin bags. I got up the next morning, rang the lawyer and started divorce proceedings.'

After years of agonizing, she had made a firm decision. But the grieving process was about to begin, and she had to deal with the reactions of family and friends. Those who were close to Kate had always seen her as a strong person who could cope in a crisis. However, after the first euphoria of being released from her marriage, she began to realize she was not coping well. She could not move on. 'I think that I was stuck on all the anger. I wept for about three weeks non-stop. I was watching television programmes and crying at them ... crying at books. The slightest thing would turn it on like a tap.'

Kate was concerned about her mother's response because she was a staunch Roman Catholic and her sister, fourteen years younger, was close to Ray. But she was surprised and gratified when her mother did not criticize, and her sister was supportive, saying: 'You should have told us how unhappy you were.' Yet she was still expected to cope and to get on with her life. 'My mother and my middle sister are always saying things to me like, "But it's different for you. You don't feel things the way we do. You can manage. You are able to do this – we cannot." I always felt that this was a drawback, not an advantage.'

When it came to their mutual friends, Kate took a practical and sensible stance. She admits that Ray never liked her having her own friends, preferring her to have relationships with the wives of his friends. In some ways, the breakdown afforded some relief for she could let go of those she hadn't really bonded with. 'Most of the joint friendships we had, I didn't really want to continue. I would speak to them. I would see them. But I didn't really want them. They weren't my friends. I didn't really give a toss how they felt.'

But there were others for whom she did care. 'The only couple I cared about withdrew from both of us. I still speak to them occasionally, I still see them, but we don't go out together. I think that they felt loyalty to both of us, and rather than side with one or the other, they decided to call it quits.' She also suspected that there was a deeper reason for the distance her friends had generated: the breakdown had frightened them, reminding them of the fragile substance of partnership and that all partnerships are vulnerable. 'I think our divorce had quite a positive effect on their marriage,' she suggested. 'It came as a shock to them that it could end as easily as that.'

Identifying those friendships that must be allowed to go isn't always easy. It is important to be aware that, just as with a bereavement, there will often be an initial flurry of active support from family and friends. A pattern of behaviour has not yet become established, but it will, inexorably. Caroline's friends were supportive in the initial weeks and months of her breakdown. Coupled friends would come to visit and spend hours talking with her, hugging her and commiserating. But, slowly at first, she began to notice that couple after couple began to adopt a new type of behaviour, and it was the same for all of them. It was as if they were participating in a social dance in which all the couples acted through shared and unspoken understanding. Only Caroline stood out.

'Most of our friendships were initiated by me rather than him. Our social life had mainly been going to dinner parties at friends' houses and that sort of thing. As the months drew on, I would only see the female friend and not the couple together. I think they became uncomfortable. Some would make a point of saying, "Oh, you must come!" when there were to be dinner parties, but I could tell it would be awkward. And I would feel awkward as well. That side of my life just seems to have stopped. I've not been to a dinner party since the breakdown. My social life has changed beyond all recognition.'

It is important to come to terms with this. The breakdown of a relationship will put all of your friendships to the test. You must learn to recognize and accept the transition and, in some cases, the loss and be prepared to move on. You must be ready to let go of relationships that your friends are not willing to continue or those that do nothing to assist your recovery. Focus on the fact that you are not losing important relationships; you are experiencing a transition that will result in your retaining some existing friendships and preparing the way for new ones.

Finding support and companionship

Few people will have the strength to face breakdown alone. We need help and reassurance. We need those who will put their arms around us and listen to us as we share our pain, our fears and our confusion. We need to know that we are loved, because this knowledge can give us the strength to fight on and provide us with the emotional nourishment to take new steps and to face change. We are vulnerable and fragile during and after breakdown, and as we move on, we must seek those from whom we can draw energy and those who will offer support while we need it.

Finding sources of support, however, is rather like panning for gold. It is necessary to learn to separate particles of true value from the worthless metals – to distinguish real sources of energy from those that drain us of what we have.

For months after David moved out, Emma was depressed. Her sense of self-worth had taken a tremendous battering throughout the marriage, and she was going to need considerable support to get through the days and weeks following the breakdown. She admits that several crucial friendships provided her with the necessary strength to survive. Her relationship with her hypnotherapist grew into a strong friendship, which was to help her face the many trials to come.

'I had very strong people around me who just told me what I should be doing and made me do it. It was just one day to the next and to the next. I was a zombie. Even at work, I know that there were times when people carried me. My hypnotherapist friend and her husband, they were just always there. I knew that if I had a bad time, I could pick up the phone and speak to her. When I had to go to the bank and sort out my finances, they were there. When I went for my divorce, they were there.'

When Robert had left Susan and moved into a shelter for the homeless, he was to find unexpected support and the beginnings of a strong bond of friendship that was founded on experiences of breakdown. 'I met up with a friend who was going through a breakdown. She was having a very, very rough time. Indeed, both of us were. We would spend hours and hours analysing our feelings and talking about how we felt about our partners. We gradually worked our way towards the notion that it was nonsense to criticize or blame them. We recognized that our partners had their own agendas, which didn't take us into account. We felt victimized. After a long period ... of talking and talking, often into the early hours, we developed a close, trusting friendship. She was amazingly supportive. Without that support, I don't think I would have made it.'

Like Emma and Robert, Kate found that support came from unusual sources. 'I was very lucky because when I announced to a friend at work that I was actually getting divorced, he had started his own divorce proceedings that same day. We were able to talk to each other about things we couldn't share with other people who weren't at exactly the same stage. People I've worked with have been very, very supportive. Unexpected people have been very good. People I hadn't even thought of.'

Early on, Kate recognized a key fact that enlightened her about the realities of the shifting landscape of her relationships after breakdown. 'The biggest problem is going out on your own.

You've lost your contacts. What I found amazing is that if you are out somewhere and talking to people, the invitations are there. You've just got to be open to them. One particular woman said to me, "It's all right for you. You're married and I'm divorced." And I told her, "No I'm not. I'm divorced!" And she laughed and asked me if I wanted to go out sometime.'

It is difficult to stop looking into the past towards the pattern of relationships we have lost or the security and good times they represent. But it is the same as peering out of the rear window of a car as it drives forwards. If we can drum up the courage to turn around and face forwards, we will see the many new faces before us.

Building productive long-term relationships

After the initial devastation of the breakdown, the after-shocks ripple through the surrounding landscape of your relationships. Over the months you will learn to discard relationships that are not supportive. You will keep what feels right for you and drop what does not. You can either rebuild your social landscape or create one from scratch. From these small beginnings you can learn to develop new relationships that give you something in return.

This can only be done, however, if you have an open, approachable attitude and if you are prepared to expose yourself to new situations and people. The process is different for everyone, and everyone must feel his or her own way along.

When Hugh eventually went for counselling, realizing he could no longer go on keeping a stiff upper lip, his counsellor guided him towards building contact with others. They explored his hobbies, and Hugh admitted he had always wanted to learn to play badminton. And learn he did, which gave him a weekly social evening. June took to sampling adventure weekends and felt proud when she discovered that people actually liked her and wanted to meet her again. Kate joined a women's group and even ventured to go on holiday, where she met many new friends. The group has planned a holiday together for next year.

William found emotional sustenance as well as many long-term friendships in a divorce recovery support group.

Support often comes from unusual sources, but you must first raise a hand to help yourself so that others may help you. New friendships are also there when you are ready for them. These new relationships are the materials, the cement and bricks if you like, that can help you to build a new lifestyle and identity.

7

Recovery

*It was like building a wall. Slowly the bricks start to
mount up. And, gradually, I discovered that there were
more things which made me happy than there were
things which made me sad. When you build a wall brick
by brick, you don't notice how you are building it.
Then, one day, you look back and think: 'Have I really
got through all that?'*

Vicky, aged 59, divorced

W E KNOW THAT the breakdown of a relationship is a devastating experience. We know that the event strikes deep into
the heart of our existence and scatters the rubble of the shattered
partnership around us indiscriminately. We experience feelings of
unreality, the black cloud of our darkest emotions and the sense of
being stripped down inside to the most vulnerable layers of our
innermost core. We know that all these things happen, so why
should we, along with so many others, expect to be able to rise up
from the debris after a month or two, completely whole and able to
carry on as before, as if nothing had happened?

In Chapter 1 we noted that a breakdown can be worse than
bereavement in the sense that the death of a loved one involves
cultural rituals to provide comfort and brings with it a widespread
recognition and understanding that the one who is left has suffered
a grievous loss. When a relationship breaks down, however, there
are no rituals and no norms of behaviour. No one can tell us what
we should be experiencing, feeling or thinking. No one can advise
us how long the suffering will last, how deeply it should be felt or
how we should react to it. After the first flurry of sympathy and
understanding has passed, there is a vacuum as our relationships
change. This brings a secondary after-shock as the pattern of our
friendships changes beyond all recognition.

Everything has changed. If only someone would tell us what to do. If only there were someone or something we could turn to for reassurance and to tell us how long the sadness and the confusion will last and what we should do to make them go away. Even though we tried so hard to keep the dream of our marriage alive, everything has gone. How long will it be before a light appears at the end of the tunnel? Will it take months or years? Perhaps we will always feel like this. We may ask ourselves: 'What's wrong with me that I can't just cope with it all, get up off the ground and start over? The feelings will not go away. What's wrong with me?'

In the period immediately after the breakdown, your grief can be overwhelming and apparently never-ending. Yet, if you could, in your imagination, be lifted above it all so that you had an aerial view of where you are now standing, you would see that the land around you was covered with pathways like those on a map. From where you stand, you can see only the few feet of stony pathway in front of you and your eyes are cast down. You manage to take one step at a time, but you may feel that you are walking in circles. When you do look up, the horizon appears to be as far away as ever and it seems as if you will never reach it.

The grieving process

If your ex-partner is still alive, perhaps still in your life because there are children involved, how is it possible to feel grief, for what is there to grieve for? The answer is that you will grieve for the death of a dream. Just because there has not been a funeral, it does not mean you are not going to be thrust, however unwillingly, into a cycle of grief. Recovery is all too often hampered by the fact that, in sorting out the tangle of children's visitation rights, finances, property and the like, you are constantly thrown into the path of your ex-partner.

When a loved one dies, those who are left behind are forced to let go, simply because they have no choice. When the loss is caused by breakdown, however, letting go is a more complex process. For the one who has been left, it often means – in the first few months at least – confronting the ever-present spectre of hope that the ex-partner will return. When will it be possible to let go? Those who have chosen to leave will be beset by feelings of guilt and failure gnawing away at their self-esteem. When will these feelings go away? Breakdown is not a momentary hitch in the flow of one's existence. Before you can begin to recover and those around you can begin to assist your recovery, it is essential to understand that the months and often years following the breakdown of a relationship necessarily involve enduring a process of grieving. It is impossible to say how long this process will last, and when you are going through it, it appears to stretch to infinity. You wake up in the morning to emptiness and a deadening sadness, and you feel that nothing has changed and that nothing will ever change.

When Caroline's husband, Tom, left her it was summer. The world around her was bursting with life. The sun was shining, and flowers were blooming in the garden. But this only intensified her pain. 'That was one of the saddest and worst parts of it, at first. We had beautiful weather. We had a beautiful summer and I never even saw it. I didn't do the gardening, which I loved. I could take no pleasure in everyday things. If I got up and it was a beautiful day, it would remind me of all the things we had done as a family,' she remembers. Things that once gave her joy now brought only sadness. She simply could not imagine that she was actually making any progress. That each day was, in fact, a step forwards on the path to recovery.

Instead of trying to run away from or repress the pain, it is important that we give ourselves permission to grieve. If you have gone through a breakdown, you have the right to grieve. By allowing yourself to grieve, you are, in effect, giving yourself permission to heal.

After William's second wife left him, he tried to avoid the grief process. Instead, he entered into another relationship as an 'aspirin' for the pain, but when that didn't work, he was faced with the full, overwhelming weight of his grief, when he broke down sobbing from, as he put it, the 'base of your boots'. Only then did he seek help in a support group, and only then was he able to take his first steps on the path to recovery. Crying is a wonderful form of release, and after the breakdown of a marriage, it is quite normal to cry on and off for months. Depression, sadness and the sense of being cut adrift can continue for some time, but after a period of months, you will be aware that you are making progress. You will sense that change is occurring, and you must help to nurture the fragile feeling along. You will find reassurance in the simplest of truths: grieving is a necessary process through which everyone can find healing, release and, ultimately, freedom.

However, giving yourself permission to grieve for the loss of a partner can be difficult, largely because of the lack of cultural rituals and because of the way in which those around you will perceive your loss. There is the small matter that no one has actually died, and there has been no funeral. There is the added complication that there is still a certain amount of social stigma attached to relationship breakdown, which inspires less sympathy than bereavement and more of a feeling that a relationship has 'failed'. There is, therefore, a belief that you should recover more quickly. In addition, these days breakdown is so common that it is easy to trivialize its effects. Everyone has at least one or more friends or family members whose relationship with a partner has broken down, and what would life be like if we had to treat all these with the gravity we accord to bereavement?

But there is something else. Many people will be uncomfortable with your grief. They will want to see signs that you are recovering quickly, whether or not you are ready to do so.

Facing outside pressure to recover

Healing is not a process that follows a specific timetable. There are, of course, stages in the process that are shared by everyone who goes through it, but every person is an individual, and each one will experience the process at his or her own pace. No one has yet invented an 'egg-timer' that can be set to remind you when you should have completed particular stages of the recovery process. You are just aware that, gradually and at your own speed, you are getting better.

To the outside world, however, it may seem as if you are simply continuing to wallow in your grief. At first, there are no external signs of the recovery, and, as the months pass by, there will be a growing pressure, spoken or not, coming from those who do not understand that breakdown has made you into a kind of invalid and, like an invalid, you need time to recover. The pressures from the outside world, from colleagues at work, from acquaintances and even from friends and family can be easily summarized: 'When are you going to pull yourself together and get on with it?'

Your awareness of these undercurrents will pose a dilemma. In the months following breakdown, you are vulnerable and seek reassurance and affirmation from those around you. You look for evidence that you are all right and that you are doing well. When you have lost control over your private universe, when your marriage has crumbled, you grasp at straws to provide you with some certainties in your life. If the outside world questions a process that even you, yourself, do not fully understand because you are caught up in the midst of it, what else can you do but question your own normality?

Months after the breakdown of Kate's twenty-three-year-long marriage, she began to hear a recurrent question. 'They said, "Isn't it about time that you were seeing somebody else?" And my response was, "I'm not ready." But I did feel pressured when my friend who got divorced started seeing somebody else immediately afterwards. I wondered if I was being silly ... if I was taking too long. Should I perhaps just jump in? If you'd fallen off a horse, you'd get back on. Even my sister recovered from her divorce a lot quicker than I did. Within a matter of weeks, she was seeing somebody else. And I can remember thinking, "Has she got more emotion than me, or am I just chicken? Am I just not prepared to take risks any more?"'

Recovering from relationship breakdown is not like jumping back on a horse after you have fallen off. For those who do leap immediately into new relationships there is, more often than not, a price to pay: the price of unprocessed emotional baggage, of attempting to avoid the grief process. If there were weaknesses in the structure of the first partnership – weaknesses that caused the fractures that led to its disintegration – they must be dealt with and understood, otherwise we will simply run the risk of repeating old patterns in new relationships. We act out old types of behaviour with a new partner without any understanding or awareness of why we are doing what we are doing. We are not in control of the development of the relationship, and we are building a new partnership on fragile foundations.

No one finds the recovery process pleasurable, and that is why it is so tempting to take short-cuts. To heal properly takes courage, and even more courage is required when we come under pressures from outside to recover quickly. These external pressures to recover quickly can actually impede the healing process if we allow them to do so.

Caroline experienced the set-backs caused by outside pressure, and each time she was aware of the pressure, her self-confidence was sapped. 'They got bored with it, I believe,' she said. 'There was a lot of pressure. It made me feel as if there was something wrong with me. Am I not getting over this as quickly as I should be? Am I ever going to get over this? I would hear a constant stream of it from other people, mostly acquaintances. They would say: "Oh, you'll meet somebody else. Look at so and so! They're out on the town having a ball. They've met someone." It irritated me enormously. That a chance remark could just shoot you down in flames.'

Those who are close to us are often worried if they don't see signs of recovery. This is understandable, for no one enjoys seeing a loved one suffer. If you feel you are under pressure from parents or close friends, try explaining to them gently, but firmly, that you need to deal with this at your own pace. Tell them that you are rebuilding and restructuring your life according to your own individual needs. Explain what is happening on the inside. Say that you know there will be good days again and that you will work towards them at your own pace, even if it appears to be slow. Tell them that you will ultimately gain a better insight into yourself, but that you need their patience and continued support while you do so.

There are significant long-term benefits to our well-being when time and effort are taken in the recovery process. It means that we are building firm foundations on which a new identity – a new understanding of self – can flourish.

When you feel under pressure from acquaintances or those who are not close to you, remember that you are dealing with people who do not know you well. They do not have an understanding or knowledge of your experiences and the depth to which you are feeling them. It is impossible simply to 'bounce back' after the end of a deep, involved relationship that gave shape and substance to your daily life. Focus not on their words, but on what you need to nurture yourself towards recovery. However unpleasant it may be, pain is both a great teacher and an effective tool in the rebuilding process. Learn from the process and use it.

Nurturing your own recovery

When your relationship breaks down, you feel that you have lost control over your own life. The pain and fear can be immobilizing at first, and then you wander around the ruins of your life like a lost child. The destruction has been so great that it seems wholly beyond your ability and your strength ever to repair what has been destroyed. But when the emotional rubble has been cleared away and when the initial waves of anger, hurt, loss, failure and despair have passed, the time for healing has come.

Beginning again means beginning with the simplest actions. Start with basic things that you know you can do and learn that you can, in fact, do them alone.

Let's look again at Vicky's breakup from Bill. After thirty-one years of marriage, Vicky's husband left her to live with another woman. But he kept coming back, promising that he would, eventually, decide between the two of them. It took Vicky four years to make the final decision to end it. Everyone who knew her thought she had been a fool to let him come and go as he chose, but during that period of four years, when Bill would visit her at weekends, she had begun to make small but vital changes. Whether she knew it or not at the time, she was making the small adjustments in her life that propelled her along the path to recovery and gave her the strength to make the decision to end her marriage. She hadn't realized that she was rebuilding a life of her own and that each little effort she made was a small brick in the new life she was constructing for herself. She spent those four years recovering and growing, and they led to a revelation that allowed her to stand back and see the magnitude of what she had achieved: the pain was gone. By concentrating on building, she had freed herself to move on.

She said: 'When he first went, I felt terrible. Then my mother said something which made me think. She told me that I had to make myself comfortable on my own. So that is what I did. I altered the bedroom around and made it how I wanted it. I put the armchair by the television and put all my things on the little table next to it. I started off from there. It made me feel as if I had something. And then I started to look at the things I liked. If I had a really nice log fire in the winter, I would look at it and think, "Now, that's nice." If I went for a walk and saw a tree full of blossom, I would make a point of noticing it. It was a gradual thing. I just kept doing the things I liked doing and realized I was content. I went for the divorce in February 1992 and it came through in November. And I suddenly realized that I liked my life better without him.'

It is through doing small things to make ourselves comfortable like this that we are able to re-establish control over our daily lives.

Having a roof over our heads is one of the most basic requirements to staying alive. Being aware of this and appreciating it allows us to get in touch with our roots and develop a sense of security. We are safe and sound within those four walls. That is why it is important to make the space our own and to make ourselves comfortable within that space. It is the secure basis from which we can find the strength and courage to undertake greater, more demanding tasks. If isolating ourselves in the home to the exclusion of human contact constitutes negative coping behaviour, being creative and productive within the home is positive and healing behaviour. It is the difference between inactivity and activity, between withdrawal and explicit action. Making the space our own is one way we can establish control over our immediate environment.

After her twenty-three-year marriage ended, Kate's home became a symbol of security for her, something she could trust and on which she could rely. 'If I went to work, I would go home at lunch-time. I felt I had to touch base. I did a lot of spring cleaning and decorating and buying new curtains. Things like that. Making it my own, if you like. And I still find that is a solace to me. If I am feeling kind of anxious or uptight, I find myself with a paintbrush in my hand. It is a way of making the house my own.'

Once we have created our own space – a space in which we feel comfortable – we can begin exploring our emotional needs. When the foundations are laid, we can begin to branch out and create other activities to structure our lives.

Learning about your own needs

Recovery is about learning to identify your own needs and to find ways of fulfilling them. It is a process of sampling different kinds of behaviour or different activities. It is a process of trial and error. Your space is the canvas on which you can paint with broad brush strokes or with fine, intricate ones. Within your space you can define what you are prepared to accept and what you are not, and to decide what is good for you and what is not. These are the first, tentative steps on the way to rebuilding your life.

It is important to know what you can deal with at any given time if you are to give definition and structure to your own life. Kate's family had always viewed her as a strong person, and they had always come to her with their problems. In the months following the breakdown of her marriage, however, she began to realize that she had needs, too, and that she didn't have a bottomless pit of inner resources on tap for anyone who needed her. 'It has been a slow process,' she said. 'But as time has gone by, I have realized that I have my own way of expressing the way I feel. And I have shocked a few people. I actually told my sister that I didn't want to hear about her problems right now because I had plenty of my own. She'd have to ring me another day. I have decided that I am not a cushion for everybody's problems any more. It is the first time in my life I have said that what I want is more important.'

After Hugh's wife Annie left him, he felt as if his life had been water in a glass. The glass had been knocked over, and getting all the water back in was a seemingly impossible task. Instead of trying to resolve the major problems, Hugh set himself small tasks, such as preparing a full meal or making sure that his clothes were clean and pressed. Self-discovery came in the form of learning to be self-sufficient and learning how to meet his own needs. 'I discovered that I could survive in the material sense. That I could manage a household, feed myself, clothe myself and deal with the necessities of life. I think this is a positive step. I don't think I really knew I could do it until I was actually forced into a situation where I had to. It has made me very independent.'

Caroline found ways of allowing her needs to expand into the space she had created. She had been with Tom since she was sixteen, and after nearly twenty years of marriage, the daily structure of her life had been torn away and she needed new forms to put in its place. Her sources of enjoyment and comfort needed replenishment. 'I indulged myself in things. I'd sit up in bed and read until all hours, which I couldn't do before. Even if they were silly things. Get whichever film I wanted from the video store. I changed my social life completely. I became closer to the friends which I have who are single for one reason or another. I started doing things I hadn't done since I was a teenager.'

Through this process of self-discovery, we move towards a stage of enlightenment and understanding. At last, we realize that it is within our power to survive and move forwards to a new stage of personal development.

Light at the end of the tunnel

For anyone who has experienced relationship breakdown, there comes the time when the light appears at the end of the tunnel, giving a glimpse of a future that at first, perhaps, we never imagined possible. When we are held back by feelings of failure and the sense that our investment in the partnership has been wasted, it is as if we are sinking into a mire in which everything will be lost. Slowly, however, life begins to change. Every effort we make, no matter how small it is, will add substance to our lives and be another brick in the new structure that will define our future lives and how we will live it.

We begin to recognize that there are moments when we feel all right. Then there are those moments when we can smile or even laugh. We find ourselves doing things we had never even dreamed that we were capable of doing. We start to regain a little confidence in ourselves. Of course, there will be set-backs and bad days. There will be times when all of our efforts cave in upon us and we are back in the mire of sadness and memories. But such times will become fewer and fewer as we continue to build the structure of our new lives higher and higher. It may seem a bit bare at first, but that will change, and each time we will recover from the bad moments a little faster than the time before.

Recovery is a gradual process. We are carried forwards by the small steps we make, until we realize that we have made it to the horizon that we once thought was unattainable. And when we reach that point, we will find a new path stretching out before us.

Each person gains an awareness of their progress in a different way. It has to do with the character of the structure they have created to regulate and give meaning to their lives after the breakdown. Emma, for example, measured her progress by her financial independence. When they were married, David would not allow her to keep her wages and he managed the household expenses himself. After their separation, for the first time in her life, Emma had to look after her own household, and her awareness of her ability to do this brought a new self-knowledge. 'I tend to walk off my depressions,' she said. 'One time when I was out walking, I thought, "Yes, I'm going to be ok." It wasn't a sudden revelation that I was going to be all right. It was sort of a gradual realization. I realized that I could handle financial situations even though I hadn't had any control over money before. I was now paying off my bills and my debts and everything was ok. It was the little things like that.'

William gauged his progress in his awareness that he had let Jacqueline go, no longer hoping that she would return and no longer needing a partner to maintain his self-esteem. He said: 'It was like day breaking softly, slowly, over a period of time – perhaps two years. In a sense, it was really after the time I broke down and cried and felt the release. I was no longer addicted to Jacqueline. In the past, things would be working ok and then I'd get a phone call from her or meet her and it would put me back. Very little puts me back now. It doesn't matter what happens. If I have bad days, it has nothing to do with separation or divorce. If I have bad days it's perhaps when my son doesn't go to school when he should. Occasionally, I think to myself, "It would be easier to handle this if we were together. But we're not." So I think, "I'll deal with it anyway."'

Caroline discovered that she could actually enjoy her leisure time without being part of a 'traditional' family unit. 'My job was the real life-saver,' she said. 'I used to love that anticipation you get for the weekend. But when we broke up, that went completely. The weekends were a huge gap and I dreaded them. I dreaded them completely. But I was fine when I was going to work. I'd go to work, come home tired, watch television and go to bed. That was it. Slowly but surely – I think probably after about nine months – things had been gradually getting better. I'd get up in the morning and begin to realize that I didn't feel bad about getting up any more. And then it just dawned on me. I realized I was looking forward to the weekend. I'd go out a few times and I'd enjoy it. Then I thought, "Well, there is life after a break-up."'

However long it takes, you will recover. You will look back, like Vicky, and be amazed at the progress you have made. The process may take months or several years, but it is not a case of the grief 'egg-timer' ringing to tell you that it's all over and you can come out of your hiding place now. If the thought of having to survive for months or years seems insupportable, remember that each small effort you make towards giving your life structure, purpose and meaning will make the next step easier to take. It is not a static continuum of pain and suffering, of emptiness and loneliness. The process will be punctuated by moments of real enjoyment, achievement, self-discovery and growth, and those moments will last longer as time goes on, growing steadily into days, weeks and months.

Recovery is when you begin to realize that life is, indeed, worth living and that, under your own steam, you are capable of creating something out of your own existence. Learning that you can make it on your own brings a tremendous sense of self-esteem and confidence, and building a life for yourself, no matter how meagre its beginnings, is like exercising a muscle you had long forgotten about. It is as if you had allowed this muscle to fall from use on the day you committed yourself to a partnership and began to build meaning into your life by merging yourself – and your identity – with another person.

You will soon rediscover your identity as an inner resource. It may have atrophied during your partnership, but it will never fully have disappeared. By exploring your own needs and by learning what you can do, you are exercising that source of energy and increasing its strength and power. As you rebuild the structure of your life, you are creating the environment from which your single identity will begin to emerge, and this is the key to the next stage of your journey.

8

Social Stigma
and Self-esteem

I did feel very guilty because, after we had started divorce proceedings, at times I wished he would have a car crash before the divorce came through. Because being widowed would have been more respectable. Of course, it would have been awful if it had happened, but it would have been a far more respectable image.

Kate, aged 46, divorced

WHEN WE ARE thrust out of the secure cocoon of a partnership there are some cold, hard realities to face. As if recovery from breakdown weren't painful enough, the outside world has some new lessons in store for us. Getting divorced or becoming separated or single again through the breakdown of a relationship isn't just a process through which you pass. When you and your partner separate, the process makes you into a different 'finished product', and, like all finished products, you will have a label. Labels are what society uses to define who you are, and after the breakdown, you will be labelled as 'divorced' or 'separated'. These labels deftly put you in your place, indicate where you belong and define how you should be treated. They are, if you will, a form of social shorthand.

These particular labels have a tremendous symbolic importance. Partnership, in whatever form, has been around since the beginning of humankind and is fundamental to humankind's survival. Throughout the ages, we have endowed partnership with ceremony, ritual, rules and mysticism, and a large majority continues to argue that the 'nuclear family' is the basic cell on which all of society is formed. Marriage is a symbol of the survival and growth of society. From the first appearance of partnership, our beliefs in relation to it have taken hold, and we simply cannot get away from the symbolic power of such a commitment. Partnership became marriage when we made it into a social contract and a spiritual covenant. The marriage vows are taken before society and god.

In this way the 'married for life' rule became sacred. For a relationship to break down is to go against the forces of deep-rooted beliefs and expectations, and the parties involved are regarded as having failed to honour the commitments by which we judge our own moral integrity. Yet divorce is common these days, and the percentage of marriages that are likely to end in divorce is increasing. Society should be, one would think, becoming more tolerant. But is it? Why does almost everyone who goes through a separation have the sensation of having 'failed'? Why is wearing the label 'divorced' all too often almost as comfortable as wearing a hair shirt or doing penance? Why does the breakdown so often result in a dramatic transformation of one's social life?

The reasons for this perception of the stigma of separation can be found deep within our culture – the belief in 'married for life' is almost atavistic, and it will take a long time for the forces of social change to transform this sense or to generate a flexibility that will accommodate the evolving face of partnership.

Socially, we are still governed by the 'married for life' rule, even though we know that statistics present an entirely different reality. When our relationship breaks down we experience feelings of failure and loss of self-esteem, and it is society that holds up the mirror in which our feelings are reflected back to us, thereby reinforcing our negative perceptions of self. We become outsiders in society.

When you feel you don't belong

When we separate from our partner, the social landscape that surrounded the relationship changes dramatically. We learn to let go of some friends and to find new ones. We learn to deal with rejection, as many friends either drop us outright or wean us slowly away from their company, and we learn to look for other sources of reassurance. After the breakdown, the fabric of our social life can be so changed as to leave us with only a few reminders of what it once was. Wheras we used to visit a couple together with our partner, we now see only one member of the couple at a time. We feel as if we are no longer suitable or welcome to share in 'coupled' events. It is as if we were standing on the outside, peering in through the window and watching the warmth, candlelight and camaraderie of our old coupled friends as they carry on their lives within.

But that is only the beginning. Gradually, as you begin to venture outside your door, seeking pleasure, entertainment and good company, your eyes are opened to the basis on which society operates – couples and families. You simply don't belong in this society now. Slowly, the message becomes clear. You begin to realize that you are no longer a registered, card-carrying member of a club you once took for granted. In fact, until now, you probably weren't even aware that society was organized along these lines and the extent to which such a distinction stretched. It is 'you' versus 'them' – you, single again, and them, partnered.

Within a year of her breakdown, Caroline became aware of just how deep the distinction was. She said: 'I am very, very aware of it at all sorts of different levels. There's the social aspect where you don't get invited to couple things any more. My social life has changed totally. I do completely different things now. Mostly with other women who are in a similar situation. But on another level, when you are talking to people in your everyday life, there is a sense of mistrust. Almost as if you are a second-class citizen. It's quite a subtle thing really. They just downgrade you mentally. You are not part of the hallowed crowd. You're not two point four children and two parents. You're different.'

Emma, who became single again in her forties after an eighteen-year marriage, put it simply and succinctly: 'You don't get invited anywhere. Society is geared to couples and that is it. If you are not part of a couple, then you are not accepted.'

Clubs, societies and social organizations are usually drawn together by a common bond. For a country, it is a sense of nationality. For activists, it is a common purpose. For clubs, it is a shared interest. The cohesive element, the glue, if you will, is a sense of sameness, and sameness generates a sense of belonging. Partnership is a form of society or club, and it is a club that has the cohesive element of sameness. One could imagine, perhaps, that the club dictates, with the same solemnity ascribed to the filling of Noah's ark, that everyone must come in pairs. The difficulty with the 'Coupledom Society', however, is that it extends across the board. It is inherent on all levels of society, within and without, including other clubs and organizations.

This is exactly what Vicky discovered when, after her husband had left her after more than thirty years of marriage, she valiantly ventured out to involve herself in social activities within the community. 'I joined a local dancing club and it was all right at the beginning,' she said. 'But I found that most people were married and it upset me. It made me feel sad. Then I joined a local women's club in the village and went to that for about two years. They were very cliquey. They used to sit there for ages talking about their husbands and children. Talking about where their husbands had taken them. I felt exactly as if I was outside looking into a lighted room and I was excluded from it because I was the only one without a husband.'

Any social circumstances that create sensations of not belonging are going to affect your feelings of self-worth adversely. If you sense that you do not belong, you feel you are not valued for who you are. What does it mean when we are evaluated by society on the criterion of whether we deliver ourselves to someone's door for an evening's entertainment alone or in a pair, as a single or a twin-pack? Caroline remembered her married friends saying to her, 'Oh, you must come!' when they mentioned their dinner parties, but she knew it was a hollow invitation. She knew that they would feel awkward and that she would feel awkward. It was not because she didn't want to go to dinner with her friends but because she knew that everyone, including herself, felt that she no longer belonged.

Being divorced, or even simply being on your own, leaves you open to victimization by a subtle form of social prejudice. Anyone who has spent many years in a partnership, only to be thrust once more into single status, knows this only too well. The breakdown of your partnership has stripped you of your title, your respectability and your social freedom. You are no longer a member of the Coupledom Society. You no longer belong. You have lost something that once made you feel secure, something that opened doors to the homes of other families, something that gave you the freedom to go out when you wanted and to the places you wanted to go, without fear of being the odd one out.

When you lose the warmth and protection of the partnership, you lose your standing in society.

Breakdown and loss of social status

Breaking up from your partner has a multitude of social implications. As you interact with others in your daily life, you will notice differences in the way they react to you, and there can be no doubt that the separation brings with it a loss of social status.

Even the very word 'divorced' still has, for some people, an unsavoury quality. How comfortable do you feel about saying 'I am divorced'? Does it make you feel good? Do you feel proud of it? It is unlikely. Most people find that the expression 'single again' has softer, gentler implications.

When you are filling out any one of the multitude of application forms that are required for modern living, does it give you any pleasure to mark the box beside 'divorced'? Try replacing the word 'divorced' with the phrase 'failed at marriage' and you will begin to understand why you feel so uncomfortable with the word. 'Failed at marriage' is the meaning that society at large ascribes to the word 'divorced', and it is too closely attached to the powerful, symbolic meaning of the marriage rite ever completely to be rid of its wounding connotations.

After her breakdown, Vicky upheld the common practice of continuing to call herself 'Mrs'. Even though she had grown to realize that she was happier without her husband, she felt the loss of her status sorely. 'I had lost my respectability and social standing, I felt. And I thought that having been married for over thirty years, I had a right to call myself "Mrs".'

Kate felt that society made assumptions about her status: 'I think people always assume that there's a "Mr" somewhere.' Caroline shared the same experience but felt strongly about the assumptions others would make: 'Everybody else calls me "Mrs". It annoys me. I don't wear a wedding ring. I stopped wearing it a long time ago. It annoys me because people make assumptions about you. They assume you are married because you have two children or whatever. I feel I now have a single identity. That's probably why it irritates me so much when people call you "Mrs" and assume.'

Most people are going to feel more comfortable thinking of you as married than as divorced, and no matter how difficult you find it, it is important to separate your own sense of self-worth from the persistent and nagging reminders of 'failure' that may be imposed on you from the outside world.

The loss of status that accompanies the loss of the partnership will, however, bring about changes in attitude from the outside world that have even deeper implications. Vicky, for example, noticed that the change reverberated throughout her life, from her friends right through to the local estate agent. 'They treated me with embarrassment. They didn't know how to deal with anybody who was apparently having to cope on their own. I noticed it especially when I sold the house. People like workmen and those who were delivering things, from the estate agent to the people who came to see the house, to the removal men. Everybody. They treated you as if, "Oh, it's only a woman on her own. Don't bother about her." I don't think it was particularly because I was divorced. It was because I was a woman on my own. And they thought they could get the better of me.'

Being on your own often means being devalued by others. You may perceive only subtle indications of this, but these vague hints carry the force of a powerful and deep-rooted cultural undercurrent – that is, that society regards it as somehow unacceptable for people to be on their own. Being on your own after being in a partnership thrusts you into a confusing social void, in which you feel lost and unable to find your footing. You are frightened of what it means to be alone.

Fear of being on your own

Breakdown means a loss of social status on many levels. As we have seen, going from being married to being divorced or from being partnered to being single implies failure. The label 'divorced' in particular has all the connotations of a failed marriage, hinting somehow at corrupt morality, no matter what the circumstances leading to the separation might have been. But loss of status is experienced on a second level, too. You are now on your own, and being on your own not only restricts your social freedom, but leaves you open to a whole range of reactions, from pity and rejection to false assumptions. It is no wonder that so many people are frightened of being on their own and will settle for a partnership that is less than satisfactory in order to safeguard themselves from being in the 'cultural cold'.

There is an important distinction to be made between the stigma of a 'failed' marriage and the stigma of being on your own. Maintaining a partnership in which they are unhappy, is, for many people, preferable to the fear of venturing out into life alone. Being alone means being vulnerable. It means no longer having the protection of the Coupledom Society, within which and by which their lives are defined. Being outside the Coupledom Society means that they are forced to define and give their lives meaning for themselves. Few of us have the self-confidence to believe that we can carve out an existence single-handedly.

Living alone after being in a partnership involves learning strategies to deal with the stigma of being single so that you can truly enjoy life on our own. This learning process takes time, however.

Four years after her breakdown, Kate felt confident about her single life. She had learned to meet her own needs and to create an active lifestyle. In fact, she wished the marriage had ended sooner. 'I look around me at some people who have so-called "happy marriages" and I think, "Well, that wouldn't make me happy." I would hate to think that I was in a relationship simply because I am frightened of being on my own, which I believe a lot of people are. But I think that has got a lot to do with how society sees single people. I am sorry that the marriage failed. But I am not sorry that I am single again. I wish I'd had the courage to do it sooner because I would have reached this stage sooner.'

Five years after her breakdown, June remembers the day she realized how much she truly values her life on her own. 'What I find astonishing when I look at married people is how they tell each other what they do and don't like. They even tell each other what they like to drink! On one of my weekends away, I saw a married couple in a pub and that was what they were doing. One said, "Oh, you never drink vodka." The other said, "I do. I often have one." And then, "No, you don't!" I realized then that I never want to go back to that sort of thing. Ever. You listen to the next old married couple. They don't half go at each other. I think human relationships can be very, very destructive.'

Where do people like Kate and June acquire the confidence to be on their own? They do it by finding their own social niches and their own ways of living amid the confusion.

Finding your place in society

When a social vacuum replaces the active lifestyle we enjoyed when we were in a partnership, it may seem as if we are being punished for being on our own, punished for being single again. Being on our own can make us feel as if we are living on the fringes of society. The entertainment and leisure industries, for instance, are largely aimed at couples and families. Somehow, in becoming single again, we have toppled out of the mainstream and are wandering around the periphery, trying to work out exactly where we fit in. This is a vital point, for it is essential to confront and surmount this barrier if we are truly to enjoy the pleasures of our newly single life.

Ask yourself to which of the following places you would feel comfortable going on your own: a restaurant, the cinema, the theatre, a concert, a dinner party (given that you were invited in the first place), a weekend away or a two-week holiday. If you have not said 'yes' to all of the above, you are not enjoying the social freedoms to which everyone has a right – the social freedoms to which couples and families have a right and to which you, a single person, have a right. Why should you be expected to give up any one of these activities simply because you are on your own?

There is no moral, practical or logical reason why you should not live life to the full and enjoy what you do. But that is, you say, easier said than done. You knock on all the doors, but find they remain closed. You feel like a social pariah. Everybody else is having fun, but not you. When you walk down the street, you can't help noticing that everyone else is part of a couple or a family. You can't even book a holiday without paying a single person's supplement, and it seems as if singles clubs are nothing but dating agencies by another name. If you go along, you end up feeling as if there's a label stuck to your forehead with the word 'desperate' scrawled across it. The thought of venturing into a restaurant on your own gives you the shivers because everyone is going to think you are a poor, sad case. You want to maintain your integrity, so it's safer to stay at home. But staying at home is lonely, and you resent the fact that you should have to.

Does this sum up how you feel? If so, what can you do? What are the ingredients of the recipe that is going to unlock the doors that, until now, have been firmly locked? What is the magic formula that will have you laughing and talking and venturing into the world again?

The recipe is simple, and these are the ingredients: research, courage, positive attitude, adaptability, persistence and more research. And there is a mantra, too, of sorts: 'If you are on your own, you are not alone.' Remember that there are thousands of people like you out there. There are thousands of other people who are tentatively reaching out and starting again, trying to make inroads into a culture that seems to reject them simply because they have gone through a breakdown and no longer belong to the Coupledom Society. Remember, too, that there is strength in numbers. We simply need to go out into the world and find one another.

Here is an excellent example of the way in which the recipe can be used. After twenty-three years of marriage, June did not want to give up going to concerts, which she greatly enjoyed. She took her courage in her hands and took out an annual subscription to the symphony hall. The first time she attended on her own – which took even more courage – was a complete disaster. 'The very first night I went, I ordered myself a drink at the interval,' she recalled. 'It was something my husband and I always did, and it's quite nice really. But I will never do it again. I stood there in the foyer and looked around me. There were hundreds of people, hundreds of couples, drinking. And I just stood there on my own. I didn't know where to put myself or what to do with myself. I could only stare at my programme. It was awful.'

Yet June has regularly attended the symphony hall, on her own, for over two years now. How does she manage? 'I developed some strategies,' she explained. 'At intervals, I either take a book to read or wander around the hall. Or I even buy some cards and find a table somewhere and write to the children.' Simple solutions that require no magic, just research, courage, positive attitude, adapt-ability and persistence.

Music wasn't June's only interest. She regularly goes to the cinema on her own, too, but she did her research. 'The cinema I go to has an underground car park underneath it. It is fully lit and manned by a security guard. I go there because I feel safe. I can walk from my car straight into the cinema. When I go to the theatre, I take a taxi so that I do not have to walk through the streets to my car at night. It's my evening out. My little treat. I never put myself into a situation where I might feel threatened.'

Kate has more of a social nature. She wanted to do something adventurous, and this would take courage, lots of courage. 'The big turning point came last year when I decided to go on holiday. My eldest son said, "Good for you, Mum. Go for it!" I went to Africa for three weeks with a group. I didn't know any of them. We all shared rooms. We just kind of moved around. It was a safe way to start. In fact, I got a postcard yesterday from one of the people on the trip who is in Corsica. He'll be coming on holiday with us next year.'

Caroline remembered her first outing to a singles club. She had mixed feelings about going but went with a group. 'When I went to one of the singles nights, there was a group of us. I sat in the car thinking, "I resent having to do this. I do not want to do this." It was like putting yourself back on the market. And I am not ready to jump the hurdle of dating again yet. It was awful. I know it sounds like I'm being really condescending, but I'm not. But I thought that the people there were a sad lot. And I thought, "If that's the future, I don't want it." However, since then, we've had fun. A lot of the places we have been to were very tacky, but we have been able just to laugh about it.'

Doing your research means finding out what is available, and it doesn't mean you have to stick to one thing, but learning what suits you and what doesn't. Courage is about going out and trying new things. Adaptability means being able to adjust your behaviour in order to keep doing the things you enjoy. Having a positive attitude means keeping an open mind and, although you know that you are up against an invisible wall of stigma, going ahead and doing it anyway. Persistence is about not giving up, despite having unpleasant experiences now and then.

This is the recipe for finding your place in a world in which you sometimes feel you don't belong. Follow it to build your confidence gradually, through trial and error, knowing that you deserve a position in society and knowing that you do belong.

If you're on your own, you're not alone

One of the most rewarding experiences of coming out of your recovery chrysalis is discovering that there are others out there just like you – other people who have the same doubts, the same fears and the same needs in respect of social contact. It is perfectly true: people do need people. Whether they are married, divorced, separated or single, people need each other to feel good about themselves. Without human contact, we become stale, lethargic and uninspired.

This is not to say that solitary enjoyments and activities are not necessary to our well-being, for they are. Learning to live alone and to gain positive fulfilment from spending time with yourself is essential. Losing a partner creates a colossal void in our lives. Our partner fulfilled many, if not all, our needs for human contact, conversation and warmth, and, with breakdown, these are suddenly gone. The greatest act of courage any one of us can make when we become single again is to face loneliness and, gradually, learn to find pleasure in living alone – that is, to progress from loneliness to being alone. The first state, loneliness, brings emptiness but the state of being alone brings contentment. Being on your own is about finding a balance between social contact and contented solitude.

Unfortunately, society has not advanced sufficiently far in its view of relationship breakdown for the finding of this balance to be an easy journey. In social terms, those who are separated continue to bear the stigma associated with being on their own in a couple-oriented society.

But remember the mantra: 'If you are on your own, you are not alone.' There are two aspects to this. First, if you are on your own, you are not alone because you have yourself, and you should come to learn to enjoy spending time with yourself. Second, you are not alone because thousands of men and women are going through the same process as you are right now. You cannot see them or hear them, but when you do venture out into the world, you will find them.

Sara, for example, left her husband after eight and a half years of marriage and started out by living in a small room. Her married life had been filled with cooking, cleaning, working and looking after her husband, daughter and foster-children. For the entire duration of the marriage, she rarely had time for herself. Leaving George led her to find things out about herself that were to bring her years of personal pleasure. It had to do with the joy of solitude.

'Until then I didn't even know I had a "self". I had started taking holidays on my own. On one occasion I was outdoors and I knew there was a lake nearby. I kept trying to find the lake. I found this road that ended in a two-lane track. The trees kept brushing the roof of my car. Off to the left, there was what looked like a fairy glade. I walked through it and came to the very edge of a cliff. There was a hundred-foot drop. There was nobody there. No human sound. I sat there listening to the silence. I could only hear the wind. I knew I would not be disturbed. I felt I belonged there. I was part of it. The wind, the sky and the earth.'

After this experience, Sara took to taking trips alone where she could be close to nature. She said it 'grounded' her and had a healing effect. In being alone, she felt whole.

June, who was solitary by nature, had decided that, as much as she enjoyed going to concerts and films on her own, she wanted to socialize with others. Gathering her courage once again, she booked herself on an activity weekend.

'The first time I went I nearly didn't go in. I nearly came straight home. I was frightened that they would think I was there because I was single and not because I simply wanted to enjoy myself. But it turned out to be an enormous success. I have been back again and again. We're mostly single, although some are married. But it's not a dating thing or anything like that. It is wonderful. When I came home, the sun was shining. I was in the Peak District and the countryside was beautiful. I remember I was crying. I was crying at how beautiful it all was. If I had never had the courage to go, I would not have seen it. I can remember it to this day. It was joyous.'

When you attempt to reassimilate yourself into society after separation, you are likely to experience the painful evidence of social stigma in a multitude of ways. The stigma is real, but remember that it is outside of you and that it comes from sources that have nothing to do with your true value as an individual. When you go out into the world after breakdown, you must become a pioneer. As you create a social environment of your own choosing, the standards by which you value yourself will come from within. You will learn that there is a world to which you belong but that it is a world of your own making.

9

Discovering Your Single Identity

Now, I firmly believe that no matter what happens in life, good can come out of it. I don't care what it is. In a sense, I do believe in the resurrection. That resurrection doesn't just come at the end when you die. It takes place during the entire period of your life. It represents whatever you can become.

William, aged 50, divorced

IF YOU CONSIDER it in the most basic of terms, it is clear that breakdown is, in essence, about change and transformation, and although that change may be traumatic, this truth remains the same: living is about change. From the most devastating to the most uplifting experiences we may have in the course of a lifetime – war, peace, death, birth, success, failure, partnership, breakdown – positive and negative events are inexorably linked in a never-ending cycle. Destruction and upheaval are generally followed by a period of creation and rebuilding, and this axiom can be applied to relationship breakdown.

The forces of destruction usually carry within them the seeds of rebirth. Whether or not you realized it, your recovery began from the moment that your partnership ended, from the moment when your great expectations of the marriage went up in flames, even if it seemed that your will and the strength to begin again had been buried beneath the ashes.

How often have we seen that when a building has burned to the ground, the rubble is gradually cleared away and a new, more magnificent structure is erected in its place? Wars and natural disasters – all forms of destruction, in fact – are followed by a period of reconstruction. When the partnership ends, the structure that defined your life is, in effect, razed to the ground. How can that possibly be a good thing? How can the loss of your partnership, with the emptiness and sadness that follow, ever be viewed in a positive light? Here is a statement that may surprise you: 'There is a flower that blooms out of destruction, loss and pain of breakdown. It is called Freedom.'

Once you have cleared away the negative emotions and once you have come to terms with the stigma imposed by the outside world, you have the total freedom to begin again without constraint and to do with your life what you want to do with it. You now have the opportunity and freedom to become who you wish to become, and you should use this opportunity, no matter how negative its origins, to resurrect your identity and exercise freedom of choice. Seize the chance to create and learn, and use your experiences as a means of building something new and the pain to develop wisdom.

No matter how glorious, and perhaps unrealistic, these words may sound, it can be done. It has been done by many others who have been through a breakdown they thought they might never survive and have gone on to achieve great things. The only limitations we have are the ones we set ourselves. If we concentrate too hard and too long on looking back over the road we have travelled, we often forget that there is a way ahead leading to the future. Before we can fully commit ourselves to that journey into the future, there is one task left to be done – to accept that we have changed and that we are not the same as we were before the breakdown and never will be again.

Accepting change within yourself

When we are children, fairytales teach us that sad stories have happy endings. Children's books are peopled by good people, who are rewarded, and by evil people, who are punished. In an ideal world this would be true, too, and there would always be happy endings. Marriages would last for ever and ever, and husbands and wives would live in peace, contentment and fidelity.

In reality, of course, this is not an ideal world. The healing and energizing power of a deeply loving and committed relationship knows no bounds, but similarly the agony that two humans, who once shared their lives in partnership, are able to inflict on one another defies description. For when we bond and share ourselves intimately with another, the pain we feel when the partnership comes to an end is harrowing. The destruction of the partnership involves the destruction of part of ourselves, and this is one of the reasons we resist separation – we know that it means losing something for ever and facing the unknown by ourselves, and this is true whether we are the one who is left or whether we are the one who does the leaving.

A few years after leaving his wife, Robert recognized the loss of this part of himself. He realized that he had lost for ever the time and expectations he had invested in the partnership. 'I had gone through a trauma as far as I was concerned. A totally unbelievable trauma. I knew that people got divorced, but I never, never thought it would happen to me. It happened to me and I couldn't believe it. I still feel it from time to time. The sadness factor. You don't go through a marriage and end it and come out without scars.'

Amputees often experience what is called 'phantom pain', when they believe that they feel pain in a limb that is no longer there. They feel pain in a part of themselves that has gone for ever. The last remnants of breakdown can be like that. The memory of the life we have lost returns to haunt us, bringing reminders and images from the past. So much of our time, of our energy and of our selves went into the building of the partnership that when the partnership is destroyed, like any disaster victim who survives and recovers from their experience we are forever changed. And before you can be truly free to move on, you must learn to accept the transformation in your identity and in your way of life that has been brought about by the breakdown of your relationship. That acceptance is the final stage in your recovery. Full recovery is about incorporating the experience into your being, so that it becomes part of what you are rather than being something that happened to you in the past.

If you can synthesize the breakdown experience into your consciousness and make it part of your identity, you will release new sources of energy, which were not available to you in a partnership because they were either drained or repressed by the structure of the relationship.

Four years after her breakdown, Emma's life had changed completely. After eighteen years of feeling controlled, demoralized and worthless, she went on to make a brilliant success of her life, but she is still in the process of accepting change. 'It's getting much better. But there are times when I do feel lonely. And days when I feel really downright miserable, but those days are getting fewer and fewer. It's good and getting better. I feel I am getting control and I'm happier. I am laughing more. People who have known me for a long time have suddenly said, "I didn't know you were like this!"'

A year after breaking up, Caroline too is learning to accept change and to absorb the transformation in her self and the world around her. 'I've come a long way, but then I've still got a long way to go. People give you the impression that after a couple of months you should be feeling better. Once they see you going out, they think you're ok, but it goes a lot deeper than that. I don't know when I'll be fully ok. But I am a lot more ok than I was a year ago. I would not have believed I would feel as reasonably happy as I do. There are things in my life which give me a lot of pleasure and I can see I am getting it together.'

As you begin to experience the relief that acceptance can bring, you become free to discover the riches that what has happened to you has given you. It is a bit like slowly letting out a length of rope, bit by bit, so that you know you can handle it before you let go of the next bit. You are performing a balancing act, creating stability for yourself while simultaneously learning how versatile you can be. Once you have generated sufficient stability in your life, you can begin to grow in earnest. It is a gradual process of psychological alchemy by which black, gnawing pain turns into the true gold of enlightenment. What once nearly destroyed you has now become the impetus for self-discovery.

Transforming pain into self-knowledge

Undergoing pain is of no value if we do not learn something from it. In fact, the pain will continue until we have learned. It acts as a dam, a barrier, in whatever area of life it is being experienced.

It is not unusual for pain to last for many years, unless we make the effort to discover the lesson that is lurking beneath it. When a loved one dies, mourning will naturally follow because we have lost a source of fulfilment in our lives that will never return and that can never be replaced. As long as we hang on to that thought, we can never let go of the person who has died. The same is true of the loss of a partnership, because a partnership is, in many ways, a living entity in its own right. It is possible even to regard the partnership as a child of the shared energy, growth and symbiosis of two people and when the 'child' has gone, we grieve for the fact that it can never be replaced.

Enlightenment is about understanding at the innermost level that the partnership was a significant period of growth in our lives. But only when we have comprehended that life was not confined within the partnership but that the partnership was a portion of life can we separate ourselves from it. When we gave a commitment to the relationship, we summarily handed over the most important possession any one person can have – the meaning and purpose of living – and when the partnership has ended, we must reclaim that most valuable jewel of our existence. When you do reclaim the purpose of living into your own hands, you will come to terms with the fact that the partnership fulfilled a need in your life but that it did not provide the only, or even the main, purpose in your life. When you accept this, you will be free to move on.

When a partnership ends, it is natural that, for some time at least, we continue to think along the worn grooves of the beliefs we have held. We will go on thinking that the partnership provided the guiding light for the way in which we live. When the light is extinguished, it is almost as if we have been left in darkness, as if the partnership itself, independent of our wishes, selected the direction our lives should take. Now that the light has gone, we must find our own way and generate our own light to guide us.

And this is the key to the transformation of pain into self-knowledge. This is the key to the future. We must learn to accept that the purpose of life was not generated by the partnership but that the partnership played a role in life's purpose.

To help understand this, try looking at history. The history of the world evolved and continues to evolve in cycles of development and growth. The cycles are characterized by periods – we talk about this or that period in history or the Dark Ages or the Renaissance. But the people who lived through any given period did not think of themselves as being part of the historical period with which they are now identified, because they could not see into the future. They could not see their roles in a particular cycle in the fabric of cultural history. They were concerned with the there and then, and they did not have an aerial view of what their part in the pattern actually meant or would mean to future generations. For better or worse, historical periods always leave behind a legacy, whether it is generated by developments in art, science, warfare, philosophy or exploration, but the wisdom must be mined by the inheritors of the future.

The analogy can be applied on a smaller scale to periods in your own life, and that includes the period of your partnership. Because the end of the partnership caused you great suffering, you may often wish you could wipe all memory of it from your consciousness. Because you will never be the same again, you may grieve for what you once were. But if you do so, you are battling against the tide of change and improvement. Once you have accepted the change, the next step is to find out what you can mine from the experience in order to reveal the valuable assets that are hidden within and thereby understand that the partnership was a period contained within the greater flow of the life you are now living.

Vicky, who hung on for four years hoping that her husband would return, learned this essential truth when her divorce finally came through. She stated it so simply that its importance could almost be missed: 'In the early days when he had left me, I used to wish that I had married somebody else. But when the divorce came through, I was a person again. Now, I look on the marriage as a period in my life that came to an end.'

Her words reveal her complete inner acceptance and the knowledge that her life has another purpose. For over thirty years, she fulfilled the role of housewife and mother. That role provided both the definition and limitations of her existence. It was her purpose in life to be housewife and mother. It was only after her husband left, and she had learned the essential lessons to be gained from the end of the partnership, that she embarked on the last stage of recovery. She realized that her marriage was only one part of a greater journey.

In the early years of her marriage, Vicky used to write poetry – it was her way of expressing her feelings – but from the day she discovered Bill's affair, she put it away. It wasn't until after she had accepted and used the experience as a learning tool that she began to write again. It took five years before she could again enjoy the act of being creative.

Robert had tried to commit suicide during his marriage. For him, there was no life outside of it and no purpose to his existence beyond the success of the marriage. Given that there was no other purpose, it would seem that the battle for the partnership was worth fighting, even to death. He could not move forwards in the relationship but could visualize no life outside it. Nevertheless, he valued life enough not to try suicide again and he valued it enough to go out into the world, with no obvious purpose, and begin again. And that was when something wonderful happened. Robert and his closest friend, who had also been through a divorce, had an idea that is now a reality. They set up a registered charity to provide support and help for others going through breakdown. His pain was transformed into knowledge, and the knowledge was transmuted into a healing force. If anyone had told him, on the night on which he was swallowing pills, that this was his future, he would not have believed them because his reason for being was trapped within the entity of marriage and he believed there was no world beyond the confines of the relationship.

The more time we invest in a partnership, the more difficult it is to accept that freedom is a viable option. It is hard to imagine that there is purpose in life after breakdown. If you live enough of your life within a partnership the door leading to the outside world will begin to shimmer and eventually become invisible. Ultimately, the knowledge that there is life outside is buried so deeply beneath the structure of the partnership that it becomes a distant memory or a lost resource, lingering at the periphery of consciousness.

For Robert, the creative and purposeful act of setting up a charity brought with it the by-products of greater self-knowledge and inner strength. He recognized it on the day that his ex-wife came to visit him at his new flat: 'When she came over to visit me I told her not to bring her religion into my home. I actually had the strength to say that to her. And that was new to me. The new me means a recognition that I have some kind of quality within which others find comfort and support. I also have an ability to look at situations and be much more open-minded. Since becoming involved in charity work, I have realized that nothing is black and white. There are always many sides to any story.'

When Hugh's life was destroyed by loss of his partnership, he said it was as if his life had been water in a glass that had been knocked over. How was he ever going to get it all back in again? The partnership was like the glass, giving his life form and structure. Without the glass to contain it, the water splashed everywhere, without form and without purpose or meaning. But there was a lesson in that experience, and the lesson was that there are other structures and other forms of containment. Perhaps the most frightening lesson any one of us can learn is versatility – that is, to allow for fluctuation within defined patterns and within specified routines, and being able to accept that change and structure must and can coexist.

If we devise a structure within our lives that accommodates change and exploration, we can move forwards without being crippled by feelings of vulnerability. This can be done by understanding where we have come from and where we are going, by taking a more aerial view of the 'recovery map'.

Hugh learned to transform the pain into understanding and to change his inability to function on a daily basis into real enlightenment: 'It took a long, long time and many, many nights. A couple of years to learn that technique of taking one step back and reasoning that this was happening to me for a purpose, for a reason. I think that, over the years, my self-esteem has been restored. It's been bolstered. And I now realize that I can say no to people and if they don't like it, that's their problem. The most positive thing to come out of the breakdown is that I now know I can survive by myself.'

Years ago, William depended entirely on his partnerships to give meaning to his life and to provide himself with an identity: he was a father, a provider and a 'good guy'. When the first marriage crumbled, he went straight out and found a replacement. When the second partnership ended, he sought out yet another. But this time, the new relationship failed to have the desired effect because, as long as he depended on something outside himself – a relationship – to give his life meaning and himself a value, he was going to be let down. It was only when he faced this and decided to learn from it that he recognized that the attainment of meaning, value, purpose, expectations and dreams must be the stuff of our own making. No other person can give these things to us, and no other person can ever fulfil all of our requirements to the full, all the time, every day, for life. We must take the primary responsibility for our own self-worth and our own expectations, and being able to live by this understanding is to know real freedom.

When he stopped looking to partnership to meet all these needs, William's life changed dramatically. He went from being a routine family man with only a few important friendships to being widely known and well loved. These days, life for William is an adventure: 'The most important thing I've learned is the key to everything else: to learn to love yourself. I believe it is what has made a difference in my life. I believe that's why so many people put up with me. Because I love them. Regardless. And I think it makes a difference. It is something you begin to recognize a good bit down the road when you have dealt with all the emotions and the pain. It's a transformation that's happened to me. It comes as a consequence of stopping and looking at yourself and the people around you.'

Self-knowledge and acceptance bring yet more changes into our lives. The way we view relationships and potential relationships is changed, as is our perception of partnership and what we expect from it. Indeed, we may wonder if we really want or need partnership at all, and at last, there is something we thought we would never have: freedom of choice.

Openness to new relationships

Your attitude and openness to new relationships will change, and you should be prepared for it. If you have dealt with feelings of dependence and that belief that you cannot live without the security of a partnership, how you view potential future relationships must change. It is essential for every individual to know that they can live alone and that they can get fulfilment from their life.

Experiencing freedom and independence does not mean you

will never be in a partnership again, and it does not mean you can never enjoy a partnership again. Self-knowledge and versatility will give greater freedom of choice and allow you to make a more balanced judgement based on a better understanding of your personal needs and a deeper insight into the mechanics of relationships and how you contribute to generating an entity of partnership within which you can live. If you have expanded your self-knowledge and if you have a more creative and flexible style of living, you will bring these attributes to any new relationship. A new partnership would also become creative and flexible, and would generate a more comprehensive understanding of self for both partners. The new relationship will offer more potential for a growing, giving and knowledgeable partnership.

Living independently does not mean that you will lose your capacity for having other relationships. It is not like pushing off from a shore and turning your back on the land in order to swim into the distance, fearing that you will never return. The act of exercising your independence empowers you to reach more exotic, complex and distant shores. You are giving yourself choices.

You can choose to maintain your independence. Relationships do not have to be defined by a couple's living together, and we do not have to live according to the traditional definition of partnership. We can choose more flexible relationships that fulfil the needs we have here and now. That is the choice June made. 'If I met and had a relationship with somebody, it would be on the understanding that he never stayed. He would have to have his own abode. I don't ever want anybody back in here telling me how I should live. Or having to put meals on the table at a specific time. I don't want to go back to that.'

William has also made this choice, and for the time being at least has a giving relationship that meets the needs of the two who share it. 'There's a girl who I have been seeing now for about three years. We have the kind of relationship where we keep each other at house's length. She doesn't want any more than that. I once asked her whether she would be hurt if I found somebody I wanted to commit to. She said that she'd be sad, that she would miss me. But she doesn't want commitment. And we've been happy with this.'

The world of relationships is no longer black and white. If you are not ready for a committed, live-in partnership, there is no reason why you should have to leap into one simply because you miss emotional and physical intimacy. More loosely defined, flexible relationships are not accompanied by a rule book, but there are some questions you should be asking: Are both of you getting genuine pleasure out of it? Is anybody feeling hurt or wanting more commitment? Does it leave you feeling warm, positive and guilt-free? Above all, does it feel comfortable? If it fulfils needs on both sides and there is no discomfort, this kind of relationship can add to your quality of life.

Other changes have to do with judgement and what you expect from future relationships. Clearly, when you have gone through such a traumatic experience as the breakdown of your marriage, your whole perspective of future partnerships is going to change. If you have done your emotional house-cleaning and if you are free of the dry-rot of bitterness, the alteration in your judgement will be an effective tool in guiding your future choices. The pain of the loss will not have been wasted, for the true gold of experience will have evolved into personal knowledge.

When Hugh married Annie, he thought that he could provide the 'bandage' for the suffering inflicted on her during her childhood and that he could heal the wounds brought on by her alcoholic and physically abusive father. He believed that a stable married life would be the solution. When he could not heal the wounds, he felt helpless and out of control. But the experience of the breaking down of the marriage gave him knowledge about himself and about the partnership, which he can use. 'Next time, I would certainly ask more questions. I would want to know more about the person.'

Caroline learned that she and Tom had never communicated clearly, honestly or openly. When she found out about the first affair, the marriage was patched up and the issue was never raised again. They never discussed why Tom had had an affair, and the warning light, which is how the affair should have been regarded, was ignored. Caroline was so relieved, and so grateful to have avoided disaster, that she felt it was best left behind. But the same problems surfaced again twelve years later when Tom had the second affair, which was the affair that ended the marriage. The nightmare she most feared had come true, and Caroline has learned from the experience.

'I think the breakdown has made me a lot more sensitive to what goes on inside other people. A lot more sensitive to their needs. I don't think I would ever be attracted to the same sort of person again. I would be a lot more selfish in respect of not putting up with problems which are never dealt with. Now I would see a person who had a problem with communication coming a mile off. You pay a price that big and you never buy the same one again. I would put faith in my own judgement. I would work towards an open, communicative relationship.'

As Robert said, you do not come out of a marriage without scars. No one suffers the trauma of breakdown without being permanently marked by it. This is an absolute and unavoidable truth. But the scars are emblems of learning. If we were encased in glass from birth and never had any contact with the outside world, never experienced any form of relationship, we would be empty, barren beings. Only through the cycle of loss and growth, pain and pleasure, do we learn. Entering into relationships with others is how we learn about ourselves and learn who we really are.

A positive single identity

During the first throes of breakdown, it seems impossible to believe that we will survive and that living will ever entail anything but pain and emptiness. We feel that there will always be sorrow for the dream that once was. The relationship that has crumbled and broken crushed us as it fell, at the same time crushing our hopes, beliefs and faith in the future. The energy, commitment and time we invested have been utterly destroyed in the destruction of the partnership itself, and it seems that those things that gave life meaning and purpose have been the very means by which the essence of our own identity has been taken from us. It is difficult not to think that we gave everything we could to the partnership and what was left has been cast away. Like the survivor of any tragedy, we wonder if there is ever going to be a time when we will walk and laugh again and if, indeed, life is worth living at all.

But life has changed and will continue to do so. You have yet to discover all that you are and all that you will be. And one truth will accompany you: you have learned that you have the strength and the power within you to survive one of the most soul-destroying experiences anyone will ever have. That strength will remain with you always, and it will give you the means to launch yourself into a new life, with a new meaning. In time, it will also give you a strong sense of self and of personal freedom.

For twenty-three years of married life, June's husband had fed her sense of inadequacy by telling her she was 'thick' and unintelligent and that she was incapable of running a household. At the time she believed him. Today, June thinks differently. Among many other activities, she is now taking a university degree in the history of art. 'I believe in myself now. I believe that I'm ok. That I have a good personality. I believe I am intelligent. I know I am a very capable person. And I feel very proud of the fact that I am managing on my own. Really proud. I am running a house, a huge garden, a job, a university degree and giving support to the children while they go to university. And I am able to do all of this on my own.'

For eighteen years of married life, Emma had never had her own bank account and she had never managed household finances. From the day she married, she had never even seen her own wage packet. The marriage ended in 1992, and four years later she was running a thriving business. For a woman who had to ask her husband for lunch money, it was a formidable achievement. She has discovered who she is and what she is capable of. She has discovered that there are no limitations on what she can achieve. 'It's done a lot for me. It's given me back my self-esteem. And it's given me something to do. Something to do for myself. And every day I just feel that I would never have done this if I had still been married. Never.'

William recently had his fiftieth birthday. A party was held in his honour, and there were a few surprise visitors. His first wife, Lyn, attended with her husband. Jacqueline, his second wife, arrived with her boyfriend. William was nearly speechless when, during the party, both of his ex-wives, together, joined him on the dance floor. He remembered: 'It made me realize that I was not losing anyone. My family just keeps getting bigger. I know that not everyone can have it that way because it takes two to tango – or three in my case. But it does show what is possible with a little forgiveness and understanding.'

William used to think he could not live without being in a partnership and that he had no inner value if he was not a 'family' man, a father and provider. Today he is all of those things, but he is still more. Of his own expectations of himself, he says: 'I want to be everything that I can be and everything I was supposed to be. And I want to share it with as many people as I can.'

This is not an impossible dream. Everyone who experiences the breakdown of a partnership suffers the same depths of pain and endures the same devastating emotions. Yet, as we recover and create new lives out of the ashes, we generate new identities that are truly unique, truly our own. New life is always waiting for us, and it will come when we realize that the breakdown is not an end but a beginning, the beginning of a journey during which we experience a resurrection of self together with the profound pleasure of reaching beyond the limits of our own expectations – the expectations we have of ourselves.

Useful Addresses

Australia
Australian Association of Marriage and Family Counsellors
12 Payton Avenue
Dernacourt
South Australia 5075

Mediation is provided by the Family Courts:
Level 3
Lionel Bowen Building
97–99 Goulburn Street
Sydney 2000
New South Wales
(tel: 02 217 7326)

Corner Tank Street & North Quay
Brisbane 4000
Queensland
(tel: 07 3248 2234)

14th Floor
Marland House
570 Bourke Street
Melbourne 3000
Victoria
(tel: 03 9604 2022)

53–55 Robinson Street
Dandenong
Victoria 3175
(tel: 03 9604 2022)

New Zealand
New Zealand Association of Counsellors
17 Corokia Place
Manukau City
Auckland
(tel: 09 267 5973 or 09 638 7009)
For information on accredited counsellors

United Kingdom
Break-up Support
Helpline: 01333 421407 (9.00am to 10.00pm, Monday to Friday)
A 'listening ear' service, providing support for those undergoing breakdown of a marriage or other intmate relationship; although based in Scotland, also serves England, Wales and Northern Ireland

British Association for Counselling
1 Regent Place
Rugby
Warwickshire CV21 2PJ
(tel: 01788 578328)
Send a stamped, addressed envelope for a list of accredited counsellors in your area

Buckholdt Associates
Buckholdt House
The Street
Frampton on Severn
Gloucestershire GL2 7ED
(tel: 01452 741106)
A multi-faceted support organization, offering programmes that can help individuals undergoing separation

Family Mediators Association
PO Box 2028
Hove
East Sussex BN3 3HU
(tel: 01273 747750)
Offers information on family law solicitors who are trained in mediation over practical matters and children

Useful Addresses

National Family Mediation
9 Tavistock Place
London WC1H 9SH
(tel: 0171 383 5993)
Mediation regarding issues
concerning children involved in
relationship breakdown

Relate
For your nearest branch, look under
Counselling in the Yellow Pages.
Provides a counselling service for
couples or individuals and helps
couples to part with less acrimony

Single Again
Suite 33
10 Barley Mow Passage
London W4 4PH
(tel: 0181 749 3745)
Offers practical advice and information
on single lifestyles and a friendship
network for those who are single,
separated, divorced or widowed

Solicitors Family Law Association
PO Box 302
Orpington
Kent BR6 8QX
(tel: 01689 850227)
Offers family lawyers concerned
with helping to reduce acrimony in
breakdowns

United States
Academy of Family Mediators (AFM)
4 Militia Drive
Lexington
Massachusetts 02713
(tel: 408 476 9225)

*American Association for
Counselling/International Association
of Counselling Services*
5999 Stevenson Avenue
Alexandria
Virginia 22304
(tel: 703 820 4700)

*American Association of Marriage
and Family Counsellors*
255 Yale Avenue
Claremont
California 917711

*Association of Family and
Conciliation Courts (AFCC)*
829 West Wilson Street
Madison
Wisconsin 53703
(tel: 608 251 4001)
(fax: 608 251 2231)

Divorce Lifeline
1013 Eighth Avenue
Seattle
Washington 98104
(tel: 202 347 2279)

*National Organization for Women
(NOW)*
National Task Force: Marriage and
Divorce
1000 16th Street NW
Washington, D.C. 20036
(tel: 202 347 2279)

*International Transactional Analysts
Association*
450 Pacific Avenue
Ste 250
San Francisco
California 94133-4640
(tel: 415 989 5640)
For a list of trained psychotherapists

Parents without Partners Inc.
7910 Woodmont Avenue
Washington, D.C. 20014
(tel: 202 638 1320)
Helps single parents develop a social
and support network

Index

Index

families
  reactions to breakdown 71–3, 74,
    79–80, 89
  support from 18–19
freedom of choice 112, 119, 120
friends 71–84
  building productive long-term
    friendships 83–4
  dealing with rejection and prejudice
    from 75–8
  fading away 73, 74–5, 76, 99–100
  first reactions to breakdown 73–5, 85
  letting go of 78–81, 83
  pressure to recover from 88–91
  support from 18–19, 81–3

grieving process 86–8
guilt
  over effects on children 59, 61
  over leaving a partnership 39–41,
    42, 87

helplessness, feelings of 26–7
holidays 106

'if only' feelings 28–30
illness, and repressed emotions 44–5
in-laws 72–3, 74

labels 98
leaving as a last resort 34–6
leisure activities 105–8, 109–10
letting go
  ex-partners 86–7
  friends 78–81, 83
lifestyle
  building a new 83–4
  loss of 14, 15–16
living alone 42, 56–7, 108, 120

'marriage is for life' idea 11, 41, 49–50,
  99
men
  loss of self-esteem 23–4
  married, and divorced women
    77
  prejudice or rejection experienced
    by 78

negative coping strategies 44, 47, 48–9,
  55–6
negative emotions, coping with 44–57
new relationships 42

openness to 119–22
as a painkiller 24, 54, 89–90, 118–19
pain
  and change within yourself 113
  transforming into self-knowledge
    114–19
painkillers, looking for 54–6, 87
parents see families
partnerships
  as a club or society 100–1
  expectations of 5, 10–13
  and marriage 98–9
positive coping strategies 30–1, 56,
  91–4
power-play, and anger 46

recovery 85–97
  creating your own space 92–3
  grieving process 86–8
  learning about your own needs 93–4
  nurturing your own 91–3
  and outside pressure 88–91
revenge
  acting out 53–4
  desire for 45

self-discovery 8, 23, 43, 93–4, 96
self-esteem
  loss of 18, 22–4, 26, 28
  and recovery 96, 118, 119
  and social stigma 98–110
self-knowledge, transformation of pain
  into 114–19
shock
  friends' feelings of 73, 78
  personal feelings of 10, 13–14, 17, 21
short-lived marriages 24–6
single identity 97, 103, 104, 111–24
singles clubs 106, 107
social freedoms 105
social life 94, 99–103
social stigma 88, 98–110
societies 100–1
solitude 108, 109
suicide attempts 35–6, 117

women
  and anger 45
  loss of self-esteem 22–3
  prejudice and rejection experienced
    by 77–8